MW00614179

Out of Bondage
Memoirs of a Sex Addict

by

L. J. Schwartz

RoseDog✿Books

PITTSBURGH, PENNSYLVANIA 15222

ISBN: 978-1-4349-9606-0
Printed in the United States of America

First Printing

For more information or to order additional books, please contact:
RoseDog Books
701 Smithfield Street
Pittsburgh, Pennsylvania 15222
U.S.A.
1-800-834-1803
www.rosedogbookstore.com

To my dad

My thanks first go to my Higher Power, whom I fondly call Papa. Next to my SAA group; then my wife; my sponsors, Dave and Mike; to Nick for all your support; to Elizabeth for all your insights; to Caren and John, who got me on the road to begin with; and lastly to the crew who made this book possible. God bless you all.

Author's Note

I want to share some thoughts about this book. First and foremost, it's going to give you the insight into an addictive person's mind. It might make you laugh; it might make you cry. But one thing for sure is it will make you understand the turmoil a person who is in addiction can go through, as well as show you the triumph a person who is in a twelve-step recovery program attains.

Medical experts say an estimated sixteen million Americans, both men and women, are afflicted with this disease. Sexual addiction is rapidly becoming recognized as a major social problem similar to that of alcohol or drug addiction. Based on a ten-year study of fifteen hundred sexual addicts, it is estimated that approximately 8 percent of the male and 3 percent of the female population in the USA are sexual addicts. But the general public, the media, and medical professionals are often uneducated or misinformed.

Patrick Carnes, Ph.D., a psychologist, researcher, and leading expert on sexual addiction, has been at the forefront of the identification and treatment of sexual addiction. He has written many books on the subject, which are considered excellent resources offering accurate information to the public. His books, *Out of the Shadows: Understanding Sexual Addiction* and *Don't Call It Love: Recovery from Sexual Addiction,* are widely suggested as must-reads for addicts entering in recovery programs.

The truths about sexual addiction shed light on its characteristics. For one thing, the sex is shameful based, generally very secretive, and it's known to be abusive, emotionally and psychologically, to the individual and the participants. Additionally, sex addicts mentally engage in distorted thinking, rationalizing or justifying their behavior. Sexual addiction is also associated with risk-taking behavior, despite the potential for negative consequences or STDs or clashes with the law. We are being accustomed to hearing about sexual exploits in our communities, the workplace, schools, and religious arenas by people in whom we place our trust. Whether it's compulsive masturbation, multiple affairs, prostitution, pornography, sexual harassment in the workplace, or as serious as molestation, generally a person with sexual addiction derives very little pleasure from the actual act itself and rarely forms any type of emotional bond with their partners. Amazingly, when trying to stop their behaviors, sex addicts find they are unable, even if caught by loved ones or the law.

As with most addictions, sexual addicts most of the time live in denial of their disease. Treatment is available to those who recognize he or she has an addiction and is willing to seek treatment. Treatment comes in many forms, mostly at patient treatment facilities across the nation or as outpatient with professional counseling. If outpatient treatment is chosen, it's a good idea to select a professional with a background in sexual addiction or addictions in general. Additionally, the twelve-step recovery programs offer a continued support network and framework for becoming a healthy sexual person of society and is highly recommended. Groups like SA, SAA, SLAA, and COSA are nationwide and have information available on the internet for guidance.

Whether an inpatient or outpatient treatment is sought or a twelve-step recovery program is begun, treatment in any form focuses on controlling the addictive behavior and helping the person develop a healthy sexuality. In some cases, medication used to treat obsessive-compulsive disorder may be used to arrest the compulsive nature of the sexual addiction. Another aspect of sexual addiction is its "progressive" component; it rarely ever goes away. There is no magic pill to make it disappear, and worst yet, in severe cases suicide is an all-too-familiar result.

This is a deadly disease and should be taken seriously. Recovery programs and counseling are very therapeutic in resolving many issues, but unless dealt with properly, the feelings of shame, guilt, remorse, and despair can riddle a person's psychological life, bankrupt them spiritually, and can potentially ruin them financially. Without help this is how a sexually addicted person lives their life.

To date, I have gone through the twelve steps. It has changed my life. I now understand why it's so important to go through them as a recovering person. My goal in coming forth with such a book was to enlighten people, those who are going through addiction or are related to someone who is.

The Epiphany

"Submit. Submit. Submit to a power greater than yourself to restore you to sanity or continue living by your own devices and surely perish." These were the two options I was confronted with the first day I was brought to the understanding I am a sex addict.

It was February 24, 2005, 9:15 P.M. I just sat up in my bed. I could not believe what I was admitting. I was a forty-three-year-old married white male raised in a middle-class home. I had my own company. It was becoming more successful each and every day. I was a sex addict who had hit bottom. I didn't know it then; I know it now. I was scared. I was very scared. What had happened to my life? What had happened to me? I was totally asleep when I was yanked up into consciousness by power greater than me. It was like I was hit on the side of my head with a two-by-four when all of a sudden, the five words I had spoken had rolled out of my mouth, "I am a *sex addict*." Like I said earlier, I couldn't believe what I was saying. It was true. I am a sex addict. There was no questioning it. What I was dreaming just prior to this was that God was tired of me wasting my life and he had work for me to do. Next thing I knew, I was awakened and admitting I am a sex addict.

This is just the beginning of a journey that began at birth. I know this sounds odd, but it's true. I'll explain later on. What I want to say now is why I choose to expose myself. It was not my will for this to occur. My will is not my own any longer. I follow a greater calling that requested I do this project and even gave me the title. Basically this is a book about hope. Sex addiction doesn't care where you live, who your parents are, what race you are, what your sexual preference is, how much money you make, what gender you are, or how old you are. It will eventually kill you. Maybe not today or tomorrow, but I promise you this addiction will swallow you whole, leaving nothing to waste, not even your soul. Somehow, somewhere this writing may offer comfort to another sex addict who is teetering on the brink of accepting their own truth. If you are on the edge of seeing your own truth or know someone who is an addict, then I hope this book helps you. It might be read by a partner of a sex addict and help them understand the intense pain, mentally, physically, and emotionally, that their loved one is in. It could offer insight and hope to them as a tool for guidance to recovery. The truth is this is the most heinous disease that is incurable, progressive, and deadly. However, there is hope; recovery is the answer.

I find it difficult to express my thoughts when trying to relate how all this began. What I found out through years of therapy was that I was predisposed to addiction from my birth.

What I did right after I awoke and admitted I was a sex addict was call my therapist. That was at 9:16 P.M. Next, I called my wife, from whom I was currently separated, and told her what I just admitted. By 9:20 P.M., I was on the phone to a second therapist, who was willing to see me at 7:00 A.M. the very next morning to talk about my admission. This new therapist was an addiction specialist and was recognized on a national level for his work in sexual addiction. Right after that call, I fell back into my bed and cried like a baby until I fell asleep. All that kept running through my head was that I wanted the pain to stop, the emotional and physical pain that ran through me like a constant current of electricity. In a strange way, a weight had been lifted from me. It was like the crucifix strapped to my shoulders had broken away and my persecution of my soul had ended. Even though I hadn't started recovery, a power greater than myself cradled me now. I felt warm. I felt safe even though I was scared at times. Then I purged my feelings, as I mentioned, until I fell asleep.

It was an early morning when I arrived at John's office, a certified sex addiction specialist. I was scared. I didn't know what to expect from him. I was only told he would see me. As I walked through the door of the office, I could feel a sense of peace. I wanted that feeling. I wanted it so bad, I would have sold my soul for it.

There was another door to go through that led into the office, which looked like a very comfortable den. We shook hands and exchanged pleasantries as he asked me to have a seat in a comfy leather chair. Once I was seated, I lost it and started balling like a baby. It was like a waterfall had opened and all these bottled-up emotions rushed out at once. I begged him to help me, help stop the pain I was in. We talked for a short period before he gave me a brochure for Sex Addicts Anonymous, or SAA as it is commonly called. Sex Addicts Anonymous, SAA, is a fellowship of men and women who share their experience, strength, and hope with each other so they may overcome their sexual addiction and help others recover from sexual addiction or dependency. John was adamant with me when suggesting SAA. He told me if I wanted to get help and stop the pain, I first had to stop hurting myself and start helping myself by attending meetings. Ninety meetings in ninety days. This is called recovery. Sex addiction is a disease that has no cure. Recovery is a daily attempt toward controlling the compulsive activities that have made my life unmanageable. As they say in recovery, "one day at a time"

I thanked John for our meeting and expressed my gratitude for taking the time with me so early in the morning. He understood how troubled I was. He was very compassionate. I left with instructions to meet a SAA group that same day at 8:00 P.M. John had said, "If you want the help, you have to make the first move." I was desperate. I finally was willing to listen to reason. I was emotionally, psychologically, and spiritually bankrupt at this point. My life had turned into a horror show, and I was the lead actor, readying myself for the final act. Looking back, I am still amazed how everything fell right into place all within twenty-four hours. First, I acknowledge I'm a sex addict. My therapist answers her phone at 9:15 P.M., my wife is at home and answers her phone, then John answers his phone and sees me the next morning at 7:00 A.M. Like all of this was predestined. I have come to believe there is a reason these things happened as they did.

The day moved forward very slowly. I had bouts of crying though out the day. I cried for the pain I have caused my wife, for the pain I felt emotionally, for just feeling so worthless. It was a long afternoon. It turned to dusk, then to darkness, and I got in my car and drove to my first meeting. I have to confess, though, this would not be my first SAA meeting in truth. Eight years earlier, while in the throes of my addiction, I was escorted to meetings with this guy. The problem was I was not going out of my own volition. The therapist who ran the men's group I was in suggested I go. I went, not willingly, but I did go. A couple of sessions later, I stopped going because the guy who was escorting me to these meetings started coming on to me. So it gave me an excuse to say, "These people are fucked-up wackos, and I am not like them." I masturbated compulsively; guys masturbate. I liked to watch porn, so what guy didn't? However, I was watching it as many as three or four times a day. I had no idea that guys who weren't sex addicts really didn't watch videos much or even at all. Not like me. I had to see it. Like a person addicted to cigarettes who had to light up every day, several times a day. I had to see my porn every day no matter what. My addictive mind played tricks on me. The addiction even back then was so strong, it was basically running my life. So I had my reasons for not going to the SAA meetings. I denounced the notion I was a sex addict. You'd think that when my ex-wife handed me an article from the newspaper about SAA meeting, I might have taken hint and advice then. No, not me. As far as I was concerned, my ex just didn't understand me.

The time had come. It was 7:50 P.M. I parked the car at this church. I wandered to the annex building in the rear, where the SAA meeting was held. I was scared. I was drained. I was so tired from the addiction. It had stolen my energy. I was like a zombie. I would walk around day by day in a constant daze. At night I could hardly sleep. It got so bad that I had a doctor prescribe a sleeping aid just so I could get away from my racing mind. As I walked inside, there were eight other guys. I sat at the table and introduced myself when I was asked who I was. There was a format to the evening, and I just sat back and listened. After about fifteen minutes of listening to other people share their experiences, I introduced myself and began to tell my story. "Hi, I'm L.J., and I'm a sex addict. Tonight is my first night, and I'm very scared."

After that statement, I broke into tears. I couldn't stop the emotions from coming through. All I could think about was the pain I had caused my wife and the fact that I was covertly committing suicide. Through the tears, I managed to get out that as far back as I could remember, I was in pain, emotional pain. I was hurting so bad, I just wanted it all to stop. It's the same pain a person feels right before he pulls the trigger on a gun resting on the side of his head. This pain is real. It's powerful. At times it's deafening, where you can't hear or see anything else around you. This is where I was when I acknowledged my addiction. This is how I felt for over three decades. I was scared. I felt alone. I felt there was no one who understood me. I felt no one could ever love me the way I was. I was broken. I was a toy, and I was broken. I was a damaged piece of nothing. This is where my head was.

The Insanity

After some time in recovery, working the steps and weekly therapy sessions, I started to trace back my addiction to its roots. One event that truly impacted me was when I twelve years old; I was brutally raped by someone I knew. He was an AAU (Amateur Athletic Union) chairman for my area. He was probably in his late thirties or early forties. I used to work out at a gym with two of my friends. We were learning how to do power lifting. Arnold Schwarzenegger was our idol. The year was 1974. Jim would come to our gym and assist with selling the protein bars and protein mixes at the meets, which were held on the weekends. Meets were held all around the tri-state area: Pennsylvania, New Jersey, and Delaware. Jim would ask my friends and me if we would assist him selling the merchandise. He gave us free bars and drink mix for helping him out. I thought we were it. This was the chairman of the AAU for our area. We were cool. This became a ritual whenever meets were held in our area. Soon we began traveling to other areas with Jim.

Of course, I now realize Jim was a predator and I was a perfect target. I had very little supervision from my parents. Even less love. I had no boundaries or even knew what that term meant. I was so starved for attention and love that anyone who paid attention to me was at the top of my list. This wasn't something I was aware of. Nature was just taking its course, and Jim knew I was primed for the picking. I never questioned why I was singled out and was asked to join a secret fraternity. I was elated. Jim paid attention to me. He set up a whole scenario and agenda for himself. I was his prize. The scheme played out like a perfect kidnapping movie.

Four or five months after Jim had befriended me and my two friends, he called one night and asked me if I would like to go on an overnight weekend trip to Delaware for a weekend of power-lifting events. I was the only one who was given permission to go; my two friends' parents said no. I would get to join the fraternity. I was going to become something special, and it was a secret. My dad had heard of this man from the weekend events I had been attending. My mother who pretty much had ignored me from the time I was seven or eight, had no input on this trip. My father, having a bad marriage as it was, wasn't focused on his children much, either. I figure my father let me go so as to have one less worry in his hair for the weekend. Football on Sundays was his ritual. I didn't exist while it was on television. So there I was, cast off right into the arms of a man they never met nor would hear anything about until six long years later.

I remember the weekend thirty-one years ago like it was yesterday. It was such a traumatic experience that I ended up getting a gray streak running through the front of my hairline. Kind of like the guy who played the doctor in the movie *Fantastic Four,* except his gray was on the sideburns. It all started on a gray Friday afternoon. It was a typical northern day: cloudy, overcast, and barren. I was picked up at my home. Nobody sent me off. No one met Jim. It was just him, me, our suitcases, and these black photo albums in the back seat of the car. There were two or three four-inch binders. As we started down the road toward Delaware, the conversation was very light and exciting. Jim was going over the activities we would be attending, then there was the agenda of my induction into the secret fraternity. I was very enthralled by this adventure, lock, stock, and barrel. Someone was paying attention to me and I was getting accolades.

We were off to Wilmington, a city in the north of the state. About an hour into the trip, as we hit the highway I-95, I was told to reach into the back seat and pull out one of the four-inch black binders. Before I opened it, Jim had told me the people inside were all a part of the same fraternity and I would be in there too once I passed my initiation that weekend. Jim never spoke about the initiation before, just about my induction and how good it would be for me. As the rain began, I took the first binder and opened it up to the first page. The contents looked like a collection of baseball cards in clear plastic sleeves, four to six to a page. The pictures were all young men in their teens and twenties flexing their muscles with their shirts off. Their pants were on. The further I got into the book, the less clothes appeared on the men. Near the end, they only were wearing boxer shorts, regular briefs, or bathing trunks. In the last part of the book, the guys were nude. My father had taken me to his health club as a child, so seeing nude men was not new. I was uncomfortable at first looking at the pictures, but Jim assured me it was okay. We were only looking at bodybuilders' physical form in it truest form. Besides, if I wanted to be in the fraternity, Jim said I would have to have a picture taken like that, too. What could I say? I wanted so badly to be a part of something. To be loved. To get attention, and here it was. The AAU chairman of my gym was paying attention to me and my desires more than either of my parents ever did. I figured if Jim said it was okay then it must be okay. He was so matter-of-fact about the whole idea of nudity. What I didn't understand was why I had to look at all the binders. After a while, the images became very repetitive. Soon, we arrived in the city of Wilmington. I was excited and starving. Jim said before we ate dinner he had stuff for me to do for the initiation.

The motel was like a long strip mall, a two-story building with rooms top and bottom. As we entered our room, it had a musty odor, which I remember to this day. The bedcovers were blue. There were two single beds. We brought our bags in from the car. I remember sitting on the bed and Jim turning toward me from the bathroom in the rear of the room. He told me to get ready to do some exercises. I asked, "What kind?" He shouted back, "You have to do fifty push-ups and a hundred sit-ups." *I can do that*, I thought. I knew I could.

Before I started, Jim told me to take off my shirt and do the push-ups shirtless. No big deal. Then I started, one…five…twenty…forty-five…fifty. What a workout. I was tired. I was worn out. Jim barked at me and told me to start my sit-ups while he held my feet onto the ground. "Faster, faster!" I remember I was getting very tired and couldn't finish. He barked at me again, "You'll never get inducted until you finish. Do them now." At that point, I started to cry because he was being very mean. He started calling me a wimp and saying that I'd never meet the requirements for being initiated into the fraternity so I should give up. I said, "No." I begged Jim not to stop the initiation. We had driven so far and I wanted so much to become a part of something.

He kept pushing me to stop. I kept pushing to continue as tears rolled down my face. Then the unthinkable happened. He stood up and said to me he had a way that I could pass this part if I performed oral sex. I didn't know what to make of this. I wanted so badly to become a frat boy. I was on my knees as he pulled his penis out of his pants and said, "I'll pass you, suck this." With that, he grabbed the back of my head and forced me down onto him. At first, I resisted as I cried. Finally I gave in and took him into my mouth. I remember that first scent of maleness move up my nose. The smell continued with every stroke. He kept his hand on my head the entire time. I didn't know what was happening. All of the sudden there was a warm, sour fluid in my mouth. I gagged, choked, and forced myself off the end of his penis. It was awful...I just cried. He was out of breath.

Afterwards, when Jim had caught his breath, he told me I passed the first part of the initiation. In order to finish the rest, I would have to keep going. I told him I wanted to go home. He said we had to eat and ordered me to get washed up to go to dinner. I don't remember much about dinner. I do remember what happened when we got back to the motel room. It was dark out, probably eight o'clock or so. I felt very dirty, confused, and scared. I wanted to become a frat boy but didn't know what the rest of the test required. Jim said we had to get rest so I'd better get ready for bed. He got undressed and stood in his white boxers, white T-shirt, and black socks. I was in my pajamas. As it grew later, he told me to take one single bed and lay down on my back. He asked if I wanted to keep going with the initiation. I said, "Yes." I wasn't sure what was next, but I still wanted to join the secret fraternity. He told me then to pull down my pants and prop a pillow under my rump. Next he told me to throw my legs over my head to see how flexible I was. I was very nervous. He told me all the guys who were in the fraternity had to pass this part and afterwards were in for life. He told me he would not hurt me and said he wanted to feel around my butt area. Soon he found his way to my anus and started probing around my opening. Still nervous, I started to cry again, and Jim ordered me to shut up and take it like a man.

What followed changed my life forever. Jim pulled out his penis again. This time he massaged himself to erection as he wet his hand with his lips and then continued probing my ass until it happened. He stuck a finger inside me. I flinched. This couldn't have been right. However, I was out of state and with a man who had complete power and control over me. Worse yet, I had no self-esteem, no self-worth, and all I wanted was to be a part of this secret fraternity. The pressure was very high for me to perform or else. The "or else" was the part I really didn't want to know. I wasn't sure exactly what he would do with me; I was very frightened as to what my options were. For all I knew, he could have very easily slit my throat. This had crossed my mind as he pressed his large body down on top of me. He positioned himself so that he straddled between my legs, which were up in the air and being secured in position by his large arms. After wetting his hands again and rubbing his saliva on my opening, he took his penis, placed it at my anal entrance, and told me to shut up. By this time, I was whimpering out of control. The very next moment I thought I was going to pass out. As he lay heavily upon my chest, he plunged himself through my anal entrance and I felt he had cracked me wide open. The pain almost knocked me unconscious. He didn't flinch. He pulled back and plunged in yet deeper until he got a rhythm going. At this point, I was crying steadily. Then there was the final thrust as he pushed as hard as he could and then he fell on top of me. Jim had climaxed inside me.

After a minute, Jim rolled off me and went into the bathroom. He didn't say a word, nothing. I was motionless. I think I was in shock. My whole body was in pain. My stomach hurt. My anal entrance was on fire. I was sticky. I couldn't speak. I couldn't feel any longer. My mind was blank. I felt comatose. The lights were on but no one was home. I was forever changed. It was as if the light of my soul had burned out. I was no longer innocent. After about ten minutes, I started to move my body as Jim was taking his shower. I removed the pillow from underneath me. It had a light brown ooze and lots of blood on it. I was broken. I was split open. I was hurt with no one to tell. I hid the pillow under the bed so he didn't see it. I crawled under the sheets and pulled up the covers and pretended to be asleep. The night was over. That was the night I lost my childhood forever.

The most damning part of all of this was that since I was estranged from my family at such a young age, I had no adults I trusted to tell what happened to me. So I kept the pain within me until I was eighteen. That was when while in a heated argument with my dad, I told him what happened. His first response was, "Are you gay?" That showed a lot of affection and compassion. Here his son just told him he was brutally raped at age twelve, and his concern was how it would look to have a gay son.

Nothing for me will ever take away the pain of that fateful weekend. No one should ever have to be violated in this way. It's just inhuman. If I was part of a nurturing, loving family, I might have been able to confide to my parents what I had just experienced. However, their lack of caring and indifference made this impossible. Also, I was sure I'd be blamed. This was one incident that contributed to fueling the fire of addiction deep inside my unconscious mind.

Additionally, being born out of wedlock didn't help, either. I was born from one woman and was adopted by another as a replacement baby she had lost after a few days of life. The lost baby was a girl. Back in the day when I was born, records of adoptions were sealed if the adoption was private. Mine was such a transaction. My birth mother signed me over while she was still pregnant. Additionally, in the early sixties, the sophisticated technology allowing us to see the child's sex was but a dream. Later on, all these little tidbits will fall right into place.

The first part of the abandonment issue I started to resolve was the one from my adopted mother, to whom I no longer speak. The second part with my birth mother I didn't even know existed until I started doing Breathwork. My adopted mother was the type of mother who showed no outward emotion. There was little to no physical contact with me. No hugging or caressing and even less emotional support. I remember at three or four, sitting on the top step of the kitchen stairs looking up toward my mother and asking, "Was I a good boy today, Mommy?" I was a slow learner, an ADHD poster child. Not that I was diagnosed then. I was thirty-four when that occurred. However, it did explain my troubles as a very small child. I was a bed wetter. Not that my mother cared to assist in helping me to stop. I was a burden to her. At seven years old, I was made to wash my own sheets since I had accidents on a daily basis. Any chance to assist me was not in her desires. Scolding me and humiliating me was more her fashion to the point of making me wear diapers every night until the age of ten. Sometimes I was just punished and sent to my room. Another fond memory at seven was when I was down by the shore for a summer. I was told not to eat candy in the morning. Well, by eight o'clock, I had my first piece and by nine, I was thrown out of the house and told I wasn't going to be let back in because I couldn't listen to instructions. A neighbor had to talk my mother into letting me back in the house.

I was made to feel like I was expendable. My mother rarely if ever made me feel like I was someone of value. I was her son. I felt totally abandoned that day. I felt unwanted. I felt shunned. It hurt me to think I wasn't going to be allowed back into my home. What she did to me at such a young age traumatized me. I felt after that incident that my life hinged on whatever my mother's feelings were toward me that day and dictated where I would be living. Furthermore, I had become my mother's whipping post. If she was angered enough, she would pick up a thick black leather belt of my father's and proceed to strap me until she felt I had received enough of her lashings. When I was really young, the back or front of her hand would suffice. I remember the summers down the shore on the beach when friends of my parents stopped talking to them due to my mother's temper and how she would beat me on the beach. I found out the truth about these friends of my parents after growing up and speaking to these people in my adult years. These friends of my parents loved my dad; however, the effect the beatings and the emotional abuse of me had on them as they did not interfere made them stop wanting to associate with my mother in any capacity even if it meant not speaking to my dad.

At eight years old, I remember going into my parents' bedroom to say goodnight one evening. I went to my dad and kissed him and walked around to the other side of the bed to say goodnight to my mother. As I gave my mother a kiss goodnight, she told me not to kiss her any longer because I kiss too loudly. I remember the rejection I felt. I was eight years old. I was a little boy. I was not allowed to kiss the one woman in my life who was supposed to be nurturing and loving me. I remember the fight that ensued between my mother and father over that incident. I was the wedge between the two of them instead of being the glue of love for both of them. It became obvious to me after lots of therapy that I wasn't the replacement child my mother wanted. I wasn't a girl. I had no chance as a child of ever being loved by her because from the earliest point in time, I was rejected by her. I was a burden. This example further explains my meaning. At eight years old, I gave my mother a Mother's Day card and I was told by her, "You're not my child. I'm not your mother." She did this in front of people. It's not like I was making anything up. Ice is cold. My mother's heart could have frozen hell.

Most mothers help their children with their homework and get ready for school in the morning. Mine only wanted to watch television or read her newspaper at night or sleep late in the morning. At eight I was cooking my own breakfast. God forbid if I made noise and woke her up. That would have been instant grounds for punishment. By thirteen, my mother stopped cooking for me altogether, no breakfast, lunch, or dinner. I wasn't allowed in the kitchen when she was in it. She stopped speaking to me about that time as well. The indifference toward me was probably the worst emotional and psychological abuse I would suffer. When I turned thirteen, my mother started spending four months at the shore house. I went to camp that year. By the time I was sixteen, she completely shut down any and all direct communications with me as well as any physical contact of any sort. She didn't even come to my high school graduation. One time while she was in the middle of whipping me with a belt, I grabbed it and looked her directly in the eyes. She knew I had enough of her whippings. Quite honestly, it's a wonder I never strangled her at the same time. Understand I wasn't an angel. Mostly, I was just a regular kid who under the circumstances was looking for attention and love. I did grow to have a fresh mouth, which I got from her. After all, she did call me a little bastard most of the time or her next favorite was son-of-a-bitch. I've wondered at times was she intentionally using these terms of endearment for me. The indifference made me feel so unwanted, unloved, less than, unworthy as a person could feel. I promised myself I would never treat another human being the way she treated me. It's not in our nature to be so cruel and uncaring unless there's something mentally wrong with them.

Today I feel nothing but sorrow for my mother as a person, her existence being so loveless from her children or husband. It must leave a person feeling incredibly empty or void of worth. Just the opposite of what a person of her age would want to be surrounded with this late in her life. Her judgment day will come, and her maker will deliver what is just.

Another part that had an enormous effect on me was the summer of my thirteenth year. I went to overnight camp. Less than a week after getting there, I started messing with pot. Most of the counselors smoked it. The older campers had their fair share, too. This I found took me away from my pain. I would forget my secrets. I would forget about my mother, the rape, the abandonment, and the pain. Smoking pot opened a whole new awareness for me. Finally, I was free. The trauma had slipped away, or so I thought. I was only thirteen. Today I know the consequences of my actions. However, at the time I was hooked. Pot was it for me. Everything felt better. No matter what my parent did or said, it truly didn't matter because I was high. I was high so much so that I would from time to time take a day or two off from being high to clear my head.

In the fall of 1974, I was with my friends I met from camp. We went to Downtown Philadelphia and saw a movie that forever changed my life. We were all smoking pot and went to see the midnight showing of the *Rocky Horror Picture Show*. Now for most people, this movie was just a cult flick. People would come in costume and act out the movie in the audience as it was playing. It was an institution. For me, it had its own meaning. This was a movie about a transvestite doctor who was creating a "monster" who was a gorgeous hunk for him to play with for his own devilish pleasures. So here I was at thirteen, high on pot, lost in my own skin, confused sexually from the rape, watching a movie about a cigarette-smoking transvestite engaging in sex with females and males. The rape, emotional, psychological, and physical abuse, combined with the hallucinogenic effects of the pot, opened my mind to the possibility that what I was watching was my destiny. I was aroused by the scene in the movie where the transvestite doctor was having sex with both the guy and the girl. For a long time afterwards, I would masturbate, fantasizing about that particular scene. Suddenly I thought I had found my calling. I was to be a transvestite. It all made sense to me. I was a guy who was made to act like a female. I thought females smoking were very sexy, and I got aroused whenever I thought about the movie. Subconsciously, the role my adopted mother's attitude toward me played a part as well. At no time had the fact that I was adopted and that I was a boy ever been reaffirmed. I kept reinforcing these thoughts about the transvestite in the movie, which kept bringing me to orgasm.

I was unaware of what I was doing to myself or that I was reinforcing the negative sexual imprint that had occurred to me. All I knew was that by getting high, smoking long feminine cigarettes, and masturbating to the transvestite fantasy in my head made life go away even if it was just for a few minutes. However, I found out I could masturbate repeatedly, so I started doing it three and four times a day.

Soon I created a daily routine for myself; I'd get home from school around three o'clock in the afternoon. I'd have my pipe for smoking pot with me and grab my bicycle. I'd ride as fast as I could to the rear of the shopping center near my home. There was a little alcove that I would go to that gave me shelter from the rain and peering eyes. I would take a few drags from the pipe and wait for the effects to hit me, which only took a few minutes. Then I would light a long feminine cigarette and start to go into a fantasy world where I was now the transvestite and the man who raped me was the man I was going to be with. I was showing him how well I turned out. I would envision myself in the same costume as in the movie. This same fantasy was used over and over, day after day, with the same results each time. I would climax. Sometimes I would stay at the same location until it became dark, chain-smoking most of the time. After a while, I had started spending less and less time with my friends to the point that, when I was with them, I wished I'd be by myself, masturbating and smoking in my fantasy. These activities led me to smoking in the bowling alley's lavatories at the shopping center. In the winter, I would go inside the bathroom and have my cigarettes and fantasy to get the same results. I felt so sophisticated in my fantasy but so lost in my reality world. I seemed to be a very happy person to my neighbors or friends, but I was truly a loner with no one to share my fantasy. This went on for years until I got my driver's license at sixteen, then all hell broke loose.

It happened in the summer of 1977. I was working for my dad. Now once I got my license, I started to make small pick-ups and deliveries for Dad's sheet metal company. As I was out on a delivery in a shady area of town, I came upon my first adult XXX bookstore. I was really curious, and that got the best of me. Now by law, you had to be eighteen in order to enter. I was tall for my age, so no one said anything. I opened the door and walked in. I'll never forget it. As I walked around, there were these little booths you could go into and watch movies for quarters. I saw the movie marquee and lo and behold, there was a movie about a transsexual. I thought I had died and gone to heaven. This was amazing to me. There, right in front of my eyes, was this beautiful woman with large breasts and a penis. I had to see it. I had to see it right then and there. I found an empty booth and went in. From that moment on, and for the rest of the summer, I went back to that bookstore, sometimes before work, sometimes during, and sometimes after work. Sometimes I did it all three times in one day. I was mesmerized. Rarely did I miss a day that summer. The fact that I found such videos was one thing. It became such a way of life that I had totally become immersed in my dual life. I was a young healthy high school kid on the outside, a sexual deviant on the inside. Not only did I see all the videos that pertained to transvestites and transsexuals, but I also knew their stage names and some titles by heart. Before the end of my summer, I probably spent over a thousand dollars on videos, pot, cigarettes, and gas.

From my first adult XXX bookstore in Bristol, PA, to the ones in Downtown Philadelphia and others in New Jersey, I found them all and I was only sixteen. I felt like a dog marking his territory. I thrived on the smell that permeated these types of stores. The fresh smell of strong cleaners used to clean the filthy floors of semen and cigarette butts. Sometimes I saw used condoms, body oils, and used plastic bags that held cocaine and pot. Never did I once think about the diseases in places like this. Not to mention the STDs I could have caught from the men I swore I'd never touch, at least at first. I had a secret, and it was all mine. It was where I came to believe that it was the one place I could feel comfortable in my own skin, a place where deviants congregated, searching for their forbidden high. I felt I had found a home. I could watch the fetish of my pleasure: transsexuals. I could get high on pot easily before I got to my location. I could smoke my long feminine cigarettes in an open atmosphere where I was not made fun of. Most importantly, I could do it day in and day out without any parental interference.

Another critical element in fueling my addiction started when I was nineteen. After high school, I had dropped out of photography school, so I needed work in order to pay the bills. I got a job at the 16th Street Bar & Grill in Downtown Philadelphia. One day I was walking to my car when this guy in a car approached me and asked if I was interested in a date. Downtown Philadelphia was known for its gay community, so it did not shock me to be asked if I was looking for a date by a complete stranger. What I did after he asked me shocked even me. I went over to the window of his car and said to him, "If you like guys who dress like women and smoke, then I'd be interested." To my surprise, he said yes and asked me if I wanted a ride to my car.

I don't remember the first night we spent together, but I recall that Michael lived in a four-story townhouse in Ardmore, a suburb of Philadelphia. I remember he let me get high and smoke, and we watched a transsexual VCR tape, whose title I remember to this day. I had no boundaries; I was willing to put my life at risk in order to satisfy my sexual desires. As I watched the tape, I couldn't help feeling like the prostitute in the movie. I was emulating her. I wanted to be her. I desperately wanted to live that life. It was as exhilarating as it was scary. I threw caution to the wind and just keep focusing on the movie as I assumed the position of servitude. I was the prostitute in the movie. I even wore lipstick and high heels I bought from a store that catered to strippers. In my delusional mind, I was a prostitute. I was smoking, I was getting high, and I pleasuring a man.

Then came the climax. I climaxed and I instantaneously left the fantasy of being a woman and reverted back to being me. The transition was so clear, cut, and dry that within two minutes, all I wanted to do was run out of his house. Pretend it never occurred. I was riddled with shame. Why? Why did I have guilt for the actions I so desperately lived to do? It was my ultimate fantasy. I had performed it my head hundreds of time while watching my videos. As I mentioned earlier, I'm not exactly sure what we did physically; however, I recall what I did to prepare for the moments that followed. In therapy it had become clear that the desire to have male approval ran so deep that I was willing to recreate the most heinous act that was perpetrated against me in order to gain what I thought was proper male attention. This chance meeting turned into another, then another, until I was thinking about being with Michael more and more. He would take me to a salon he had a key to and would make me lie on one of the massage tables in a submissive position on my back and force rectal entry while calling me "slut" and "whore." Names I thought I cherished to hear from a loving person. Then after each episode, I would again revert back to my male self, never allowing him to touch me. I was truly living a dual life. I had a girlfriend I was living with, and I was acting out with Michael when my addiction would take over. He was like a magnet drawing me toward him. When I was in that place, nothing else mattered. I would focus on just the fantasy of being in my role as a transvestite. Even though Michael would verbally abuse me, I sought out his desires anyway, regardless if I wanted to be there or not. I knew he was only using me, and I didn't care because I had my own agenda.

As the months turned into years of seeing him, I would see a pattern show up that would be the same for every relationship I would have in the future. It was all about me. I didn't care for him. I only cared that I could come over, get high, dress up, smoke my feminine cigarettes, watch transsexual videos, and do as I chose to do with Michael. I acted extremely domineering as I became even more selfish. Michael liked this, and I became more confused as to who I was. On one hand, I was this male dressing up to look female, and then there was my male side that always appeared the moment I climaxed. I would become riddled with shame and guilt from my actions. What kind of monster was I becoming? I was without shame one moment, then crying over my actions the next moment. What was constant in all my relationships before and after Michael was that no matter who I was dating at the time or living with, I had these divided personalities going on. My exploits had progressed to having anal sex I despised, but I kept letting him do it to me. The whole situation got out of hand when he started calling other men for me to be with while he watched. My addict inside me was thrilled. I was finally becoming the prostitute I dreamed of. This is progression. Like they say in the recovery rooms, this disease is incurable, progressive, and deadly.

One time Michael told me to stop fooling myself and to just admit I was gay and to tell my girlfriend that I was leaving her for him. This presented two problems. One, if I was gay, why would I have so much shame regarding my activities with Michael? Number two, I never felt in my heart that I was attracted to men. I couldn't explain why I was with them. I just was and kept repeating my actions more and more often as I got older.

In 1984 I took another job that further fueled my addiction. At twenty-four, I became a male stripper, a Chippendale type who did revues. I figured, why not? I had the build since I still actively worked out. What really got me into it was a night at a bar where they were having a contest for hot bodies. The prize was a hundred dollars. I looked at the competition that went out onto stage that night and I said to myself, *I can beat those guys.* So the following week, I went back to the same bar and entered the contest. The only difference was I stopped off at the same lingerie store I bought my heels and picked up a g-string with a gold tassel hanging down in the center, which I was able to twirl as I gyrated my hips. As fate would have it, I won the contest hands down and my stripping career was started. So not only was I going to the adult XXX bookstores; I was now into exhibitionism. I never thought of myself as an exhibitionist.

After five years in the business, I did over three thousand performances, and I prided myself on never getting involved with anyone for whom I performed. The funny thing was I had the integrity not to mix work with pleasure, but I thought nothing about going to an adult XXX bookstore and having anonymous sex. I find that pretty ironic. Additionally, since I portrayed this wholesome male, no one would ever had suspected I had this dual life. I presented myself as this moralistic individual when in reality, I had no scruples whatsoever. I lived in a world of shame and pain on the inside and never let on that I had this pain deep in my gut. In 1989, after I retired, I started to write about my career in stripping; however, it was boring since I never had any affairs with anyone. Unlike real rock-n'-roll stars and their groupies, I lived a quiet life as a stripper. Although my dark side was anything but dull, I thrived on the chaos.

Going back, in 1986, while in full-blown addiction, I met a girl who was a wholesome-type Plain-Jane beauty. We dated while I was a stripper. She had two daughters. We all got along great, but the relationships were superficial. It was though I was playing this role of boyfriend instead of being a true boyfriend. One thing led into another as I steered the relationship on a course I wanted it to go. After all, I was only looking at the relationship from the aspect of what was I getting from it, not what was I contributing to it. I didn't understand what love was. I didn't understand what real romance was. I used my body and smooth talk to paint pictures of perfect harmony when in reality, it was a show of smoke and mirrors. I truly believed I was nothing more than a conman. This relationship worked until I started asking for sexual pleasures that were not in the normal realm of our relationship. The truth was I had crossed the line with my dark side, and it wanted fulfillment in my perfect world at home. I became agitated when I wasn't getting the type of pleasure I had requested. My addiction wanted to "feed" not only when I was alone, but it also wanted to be "fed" at home now. I couldn't understand why my girlfriend was opposed to inserting a dildo into me rectally. In a "normal" relationship, where two people play as one and romance is shared between two hearts, experimenting is not so far out of the question. However, I blindsided her. One day my desire was not there, then the next day it was. Not to mention that I was so caught up in going to the adult XXX bookstores, any sexual attempts on her part were shut down due to my guilt and shame. The relationship only lasted two years before she finally called it quits. I was out of control in my addiction, so I had a comfort zone I could retreat to for warmth and solace. That comfort was found at the adult XXX bookstores, getting high and working more than ever. I wasn't ready to mourn another lost relationship just yet. I needed to keep from feeling as best I could. I moved out.

One day in 1986, after I had broken up with my girlfriend, I was at my agent's office when his telephone rang. He was in the bathroom and I was the only one in the office. So rather than lose a call, I answered the phone very professionally and a woman was on the line. She asked for the owner, and I mentioned he was out of the office for a moment. Instead of just taking a message, I asked if she needed assistance. She was making an inquiry of stripping business and was looking for a stripper to do a private party. I immediately became flirtatious and started sexualizing almost everything she said. As it turned out, what she was looking for was a person to play sexually with her and her boyfriend. Since Mark, my agent, wasn't in the office and I knew this type of conversation wasn't anything that Mark would have entertained, I asked for her phone number and told her I would call her right back. Talk about living on the edge. I had just gotten the ultimate gift fall right into my lap. Free sex. I was in heaven.

I was in a trance. I didn't know these people. I didn't care. I was so pumped with adrenaline thinking about this woman. I told her I liked it kinky, and she fell right into my conversation. What I didn't know was, who was she? Ten minutes later, I left the office and went to a pay phone and called her back. She was very sexual when I called back. We instantly had a connection. It was all sexual. What she was looking for was a slave boy to service both her and her friend. She played the part of a dominatrix and liked to watch a slave boy serve her every whim. I lied and told her I had experience and was willing to do whatever she wanted. Finally she gave me instructions to meet her at an empty parking lot of a church near where I lived. She told me to look for a silver minivan with tinted windows. She gave a time to meet her. I hung up, saying, "Yes, Mistress." I was in a deeper trance than before I was so deep in my addiction, there was no one or anything that would have stopped me from going.

It was about one or two o'clock—I don't remember exactly—but I do remember it was right after lunch. With butterflies in my stomach and cotton mouth, I pulled into the church parking lot as instructed. A silver minivan pulled in the lot just like she said it would and parked right next to me. Crazed with anticipation, I got out of my car and the passenger-side window rolled down. I was shocked. There in the passenger seat was an attractive dirty blonde woman around thirty, with a short dark-haired guy who was driving. He looked like a computer geek with his horn-rimmed glasses. I introduced myself and her first words were a directive, "Shut up and get in the back." Without question the adrenaline rush scale just blew off its top. I followed her comment with a "Yes, ma'am" as I opened the side door of the minivan. There was no rear seat. The driver got out and came around and told me to sit Indian style and to put my hands behind my back. I was so turned on at this point I did as I was told. Next thing I felt was tape being placed over my wrists, which were now behind me. He then put a blindfold over my face so I couldn't see where I was being taken.

Now any person with half an ounce of smarts would never have allowed themselves to be placed in this predicament. I, on the other hand, am an addict. It was a dangerous scenario for sure, and I was so entranced I never thought about danger or the value of my life. All I wanted was to play sexually. There were no boundaries I wasn't willing to cross.

After a while, the car pulled up to a stop, the engine was shut down, and I was told to get ready to exit. I heard the sliding side open, and I was guided to the ground and told to walk. The geek had a hold of my arm and walked with me through the front door. I didn't know where I was. The blindfold was removed, and I found myself standing in a condo foyer. I didn't recognize what complex I was in. It didn't matter. All that mattered was the "game" with which I was involved. I manipulated this woman into having me at her house, and now she wanted her due. Her first orders after my wrists were freed were to strip naked in front of her. I did as she demanded. There I stood in front of this man and woman I only met an hour before, completely naked. She looked at my body and made cruel statements to the effect that I was less than as a man. Even if I was built then, she humiliated me to the point of wanting to run away. However, I was turned on in a weird sort of way. This woman was abusing me verbally, and I was attracted to her like a moth to a flame on a hot summer night. She told me to lie on the floor with my stomach facing up and to spread my legs out and lift them off the floor. I did as I was told. She whispered something in the guy's ear and off he ran to the other room, returning with K-Y lube and a butt plug the thickness of my wrist. Just then I felt my first sense of fear. I was told to lube up the plug and insert it. From the size of the plug, I knew I couldn't get it into me. This was something someone would use as a prep before taking a fist. I was not into fisting, but I didn't know if these two were. I started to become fearful as I entered the tip of the plug into my rectum. I felt pain almost instantly. I grew more nervous. Then all at once, I heard the degrading comments of what a useless bitch I was because I couldn't get the plug in any deeper.

"Mistress" gave me one more chance to prove I was worthy of her time by getting the plug completely inside me. I knew I was not going to make it in. I tried again as hard as I could. My lie had finally caught up with me, and she knew it. She called me a worthless piece of shit for wasting her time. I was told to get dressed and to get out of her sight and get out of her house. By this time, I had snapped out of my "high" and felt less than a man. I was so ashamed of what I had tried doing and felt extreme guilt. I was again blindfolded and put back into the car. My hands were not tied up this time. The ten-minute ride felt like an hour. The geek drove me back to the parking lot as he was told. After he parked to let me out, I won't forget how he told me get a life and fuck off. Today, through the clarity, I am amazed at the fact that I had such little care for my own wellbeing. I could have been killed. I could have been raped. I could have been tortured. They could have poured gasoline over my body and lit me on fire. The truth was I was in addiction and knew no boundaries, only lies, deceit, and manipulation. I was very lucky that day.

Today it's a different story. Today I'm in recovery. If it wasn't for the grace of God, I would not be alive today. However, my misery back in the eighties wasn't over the day I was thrown out of the couple's house. It was only a matter of time before I was back watching videos the very next day.

By this time, I was living with a guy named Marc I had met who had a store next to my ex-girlfriend's store. This guy's business was all about being with strippers. He had a fingernail supply business and personally did the nails for a lot of the strippers. I loved it. He even had the Penthouse Pet of October stay with us a few nights. She was going to be a roommate. I was loving this idea. Although I couldn't ever share my true identity with her, I did have fantasies about her and us being the perfect partners. What a delusion. I just continued to get high every day and strip. Then one day at Marc's store, this doctor came in with his stepdaughter to form a partnership with Marc, making him a distributor for a personal hair care and skin care company. They had a product that today has been called a success for growing hair. The thrill for Marc was he had a bald spot he hated and was looking to get help growing hair.

The stepdaughter and I hit it off. She talked about her products, and I talked about my failed relationship. Then she excused herself to have a cigarette, and she pulled out of her purse the same feminine brand I smoked. I was instantly smitten. I never said anything about them—that was my secret, and once again my addiction snapped into action. That day alone, we spoke until two or three in the morning. The next day, we made arrangements to meet up and chat some more. I learned about the skin and hair care products as well as the business opportunity and became interested in the company. Again, we spoke until wee hours of the night. As was the pattern of my relationships, I quickly became attached to this woman. Her name was Laurie. She would eventually become my first wife. We talked days and nights and since I was a professional stripper, my time was basically my own.

It was summer of 1987. Laurie and I continued to see each other every day. She would come visit me at my place and vice versa. We didn't have sex at first because I was setting her up to fall for me, in my delusion-addicted mind. I told her that my former girlfriend didn't understand me and I was tired of sex. I hated it and wasn't interested in having it with just anyone. Then it happened one night while at Laurie's parents' house. Laurie at that time slept on a mattress on the floor. We were talking, I remember it was another late-night conversation. One thing led to another, and we went from friends to lovers. That was how it began. We didn't regret doing it. It didn't stop me from going to the bookstores or from stripping. What it did was begin another relationship. I thought it was love, but in fact, it was based on a lie. I know this now because of my recovery. It has allowed me to see clearly how I equated sex with love. In reality intimacy forges love, which may or may not lead to loving sexual relations. I can see that now and am grateful my recovery has given me the gift of clarity.

As the time marched on, Laurie and I decided to move in together. She like creating gift baskets as a way to earn extra money, and adding "stripper" to her product line was a sure bet to make even more money. Laurie became my "pimp" of sorts and hired me out to private parties, "Stripper for Hire." From time to time, she would ride with me to the shows and wait in the car as I did my performances. I appreciated the company but soon learned it cramped my style. My addiction wasn't free to go as it pleased. I soon made it a point to go alone, once more allowing me the freedom to stop in at my favorite adult bookstore haunts. The relationship seemed to cruise along at an even pace, so we decided to marry. We got married right there in our kitchen. Her uncle, a notary, did the honors over a bottle of wine, and we said our "I do's" and made it official. Needless to say, her parents were not at all pleased. I was a "nothing" in their eyes, a nobody, and they never missed an opportunity to let me know it. It was January 11, 1988.

So there we were, a sex-addict stripper in active addiction married to this strong-willed woman who made no bones to say what was on her mind. What once was a nice little romance had become a dictatorship. And it was her mother who ruled. If I came home late from doing a show, her mom knew. If I made good money, her mom knew. If we disagreed on something, her mom knew. It was not the recipe for a happy marriage. I started lying terribly, and after a few months, the sex started to dry up to nothing. I had no interest. I had shame and guilt, so I wasn't joyful with my partner. We started to argue a lot. It would get loud and vicious. Name calling got flung around like mud. There was a great deal of pain associated with what was occurring. There was little communication at times and once again, her mother knew everything. I didn't have the guts to move out. The fights got worse. The communication drifted to almost nothing. The love had dried up. Once again I had driven someone away. The lies, the deceit, and the manipulation had all come crashing down on me. Then one day just before our two-year anniversary, I walked into the condo her parents bought for us and her mother turned and suggested we separate. Finally, relief. I took my clothes and moved into a house of a couple I never knew. They were a couple, an acquaintance of mine who had a room for rent. So I took up the offer. I moved out.

It's a funny thing, but considering my addiction status at the time of my first marriage, I remember very little from it. In a lot of ways, Laurie reminded me of my mother. She was verbally abusive and a strong-willed individual. I was comfortable with this type of abuse. It was what I was used to. Since I had very low self-esteem and self-worth, I thought I deserved the abuse I was getting. I can say that I am grateful to my ex-wife for one thing that changed my life for the better. She suggested I go to work at American Express in Plantation, FL. However, I met my current wife while I was working there. A gift she gave me that keeps on giving. I really must have been a bastard in the last months while married. As I mentioned, I really don't remember much. It was Laurie who first handed me a clipping out of the newspaper for an SAA meeting downtown in Ft. Lauderdale. I took the clipping and threw it away. It's funny, she was right on target. It really didn't matter much. I was in such denial. I couldn't face the idea that I was a sex addict.

This was another chapter of broken relationships. Our first night apart, I remember crying in my bed at night, wanting to go back. I was just starting to feel the real pain of my broken relationship when I would go anesthetize myself once again. Fortunately for me, I had some people I knew who didn't really know the real me but who thought I was a decent guy. One person in particular was a guy named Scott. He had some friends who had a house and opened up their house to boarders. I needed a place to live since I was now out on my own again. The couple, Tony and Martha, were a sweet couple. They were younger than me. They tried to make my stay as homey a possible. I had my own bathroom and bedroom. They would ask me to eat dinner with them, too. I really appreciated their warmth and family attitude. I was like an older brother. We were all kids, really. Tony had his own business, and Martha was in a related business where working together as a team was the course of each week's events. It's safe to say Tony was the brawn to Martha's brains. I really grew fond of them over time. But I never let them see the real me, only who I wanted them to see. I had to be "perfect" in how my life was. The funny thing was that Tony was an internet porn freak and loved to show things to me all the time. I believe he was a sex addict, too. Meanwhile, I was in complete agony. I left my marriage. I questioned my sexuality on a daily basis. I continued going to bookstores and gave into being a transvestite. I was estranged from my father, who lived three miles from me. To him my failed marriage was just another strike against me.

That's all I was to my dad. Just a failure. No promise of ever amounting to anything. So it was no wonder I had a strained relationship with him as well. At this point in my life, even I felt like a failure. I turned to the one comfort I knew I hated and loved at the same time. I would get high and sit in the small movie booths in the adult bookstore and masturbate until at times I bled. It's not the bleeding that was the bad part. It was the delusion that I was supposed to be a transvestite and that my life was supposed to revolve around sex. I sexualized everything, everyone, and did it unconsciously.

I did have one shining spot at that time. That was a friendship I had with my current wife, Lainie. She was still married to another man and worked at American Express. I liked her from the start. But it would be a while before our relationship would blossom. Soon after I had moved away from my first wife, I received a call asking me to meet her at an attorney's office. It had been a month since my wife and I had spoken. She wanted a divorce. Truth be told, her requesting a divorce probably saved my life. There is no telling where my addiction would have taken me back then. I was definitely not right for that woman nor was she right for me. About a month and a week after we separated, I was a divorced man, once again on my own in life. I had all of my druggie and sexual liaison friends who I thought were my "true" friends to help get me through. So in my delusion, I wasn't alone at all.

This time alone allowed me to stretch in other areas of my life. The year was 1990. I started thinking about my future. I jumped around a lot with jobs. I would always have one scheme or another to make money. I didn't go to college very long, so I never got a degree. I had all these grandiose ideas for making money. I did the 900 numbers with the girls who chatted sexually. I wanted to create a website that sold sex toys and novelties. I even thought about opening a club catering just to transsexuals and transvestites. I tried telling a friend of mine that it was such a cool idea. She never got into it, and I never understood why. I thought I had a cool idea for making money. Today through my recovery, I know differently. I know all those activities were just extensions of my addiction and justification for being able to act out.

I eventually fell into the cabling industry. I always liked playing with wires and electronics when I was younger. I took a position as a helper for a cable television installation company. This proved to be a good move for me. At the same time, my addiction went into hibernation. I had little time to go to the bookstores or dress up since I was living with this couple. Then one day in 1990, I ran into my friend from American Express. She had left her husband. They had a very bad marriage. She was abused emotionally and he had been violent—never hitting her but busting up things around the house. She was scared. He couldn't control his temper. Even though many months had passed since we'd seen each other, it was as if we hadn't skipped a beat of time. We talked for a long time, and I asked her to get together for dinner. It wasn't a date, really; we we're just friends. As usual we played cards and just talked. There was one difference; for whatever reason, I opened up and told her about myself. I was saying that the next person I met, I wasn't going to hide who I was. She didn't understand what I meant. "What do you mean, hide who you are?" she said. Then I spilled the beans. I told her I liked to dress up and live as a transvestite. There was silence. Then there was more silence. Then a smile came upon her face, and she said that was sort of sexy. I told her I liked to smoke feminine cigarettes and wanted to be the "best girlfriend" to my girlfriend a girl could ever know. The smile got bigger. Once again a secret world opened up for me. But this time, I brought someone into my world with me.

Soon after our little talk about my "secret life," our friendship grew deeper. We were talking every day. She was living in an apartment complex near me and had a new job in a mall not far as well. I asked her out on a date. I had the coolest place I wanted to take her. It was a surprise. First we had dinner, and then I told her we needed to take a car ride. I had that special place I wanted to show her. After twenty-five minutes of driving, I pulled into the back of the dumpy little commercial building. The outside was faded chipped white paint with a sign on the door. The sign read, ADULT MATERIALS INSIDE. MUST BE OVER 18 TO ENTER. At this point, I was in a drug-like trance, I was so high. Here I had a female friend I liked getting ready to enter an adult bookstore I frequented almost on a daily basis before I got my cabling job.

As the door creaked open, that smell of ammonia cleaner rolled past my nose, an all-too-familiar smell. I held open the door, and I had Lainie walk in first. I was mesmerized at how open she was to going in. On the right-hand side were rows of videos from floor to ceiling. On the left-hand side were magazines from floor to ceiling. As we walked down this aisle, it opened up into a great room with rows of videos everywhere. Every kind you could imagine. From bondage and discipline to multiple gangbangs, black and blondes, to my favorite: transsexual sex. There were the adult toys, which we couldn't stop laughing at, and blow-up dolls.- To the far right in the great room surrounding the perimeter were the video booths, which showed multiple videos on a timer all for a buck a play. On the wall before the booths was a board showing all the videos the booths were currently playing. On this marquee, it had over thirty choices of viewing. I was so excited to show Lainie the board. It was like a hunter showing off his kills. My eyes were probably glassy from the high.

We looked over the board and laughed over some of the titles. I pointed out the transsexual titles and told her she had to check out the videos. I walked over to one of the booths and opened the door. On the floor there were cigarette butts and semen and saturated towelettes—the smell was all too familiar to me. Lainie had a look of disgust on her face. We open a few other booths until we found one that was clean or at least cleaner than the others. I told her to sit down in the seat as I entered a few dollars into the player. I never once thought about how unsanitary this place was, who might have seen us come in, or whether or not the place was getting raided by the police. I had such tunnel vision. I was crazed. We stayed there for about an hour or so. As I look back, I realize this was my first date with this woman. I was insane to think this was an appropriate place to take her. It was a filth hole. We went back to the house, where I stayed and shared the news with my roommates, and all had a good laugh.

Activities like that were uncommon. We only went once. But soon we were getting together a lot—and frequently went to an adult video store by my house and rented a transsexual video, as we had gone from just being friends to becoming lovers. Even though I had my job with cabling and didn't frequent the adult bookstores any longer, the activity of watching the videos when we were making love continued my addiction. Additionally, I had Lainie helping me with make-up and she started to smoke the feminine cigarettes I used. I may not have been going to the bookstores, but I did still put on lip gloss and smoke as I masturbated to the fantasy of the transsexual videos almost on a daily basis. I didn't think at that time how this behavior was affecting this blossoming new relationship. As far as I was concerned, we had a good thing going. I thought she liked my little quirks. Nothing could have been further from the truth, I would find out later—years later, to be exact.

So the relationship blossomed into love. After six months, we got an efficiency apartment together and set up house. From there I asked for her hand in marriage almost two years after I divorced. She accepted and we got married in the summer of '91. It was a beautiful wedding. It was very small. Only Lainie's family showed up. I asked my parents to come; however, my father told me my mother wouldn't come because we picked a date when it inconvenienced my mother. My mother sure had a busy schedule. My father wasn't able to make it alone because of the repercussions my mother would have given him. It didn't matter; Lainie's family more than made up for the family I didn't have. It was a beautiful ceremony. A sun-filled Sunday morning under a one hundred-year-old huppa. Our affair was held at the world-famous Fountainbleu Hotel on Miami Beach.

Like a true newlywed, I even carried her over the threshold at the apartment, and our love nest blossomed. I still masturbated every day and made it a point to do it in the apartment in the bathroom with lip gloss on so it would show up on my cigarette. Even though my addiction was in low gear, it still manifested itself, keeping its claws deep in my soul. Right before we got married, I got an inside position with a local cable company. I no longer had to worry about having my own truck or paying for my tools. I was an employee, an inside guy. They gave me a truck, uniform, route, and benefits. I only needed to show up on time. I did really well and started to get recognized for my good work. But of course, this couldn't last.

A few months into our marriage, I started getting into phone sex. My schedule would put me at addresses where people lived in apartments. Small, medium, or large, it didn't matter. These were called MDUs, Multi-Dwelling Units. The one thing they all had in common was each had a meter room, which housed the phone switch where all the wires connected for all of the phones in the complex. This allowed me to use a patch phone that the telephone company guys used for their service work. I bought one at the flea market for forty bucks. It looks like a telephone receiver with a wire coming out one end. This wire has two alligator clips that can attach onto the terminals of anyone's phone line. It has a keypad on one end that allows you to touch-tone dial anywhere in the world. This was a great tool for the phone company and serious addict's toy for phone sex. I called a lot of numbers when I was supposed to be working. I called all kinds of phone sex services. I did it for a period of time until I got paranoid I was being watched. I would hook up to a call, masturbate, and smoke all at the same time. I got so hooked, I couldn't stop. I was afraid I was going to get caught by a coworker or the telephone people. I tried stopping, but the rush kept me going. Then one day, I just stopped. I really don't know how I did it. I just know I was so paranoid, I guess the fear of God made me stop. Eventually, I sold that little handset to one of the other guys at my job. Those actions could have put me in jail. It would have been considered federal charges against me since the telephone company is in more than one state. By the grace of God, I was saved without any harm coming to me other than that I did against myself.

After that episode, I laid low from any activities except for the smoking at home and watching videos with my wife. It was hard to put down the phone sex; I'm so turned on by verbal communications. I'm also very visual, a voyeur, for sure. It's no wonder I loved videos so much that had a lot of verbal talk. I'm glad I never got into the internet porn; where you could see the person you could talk to and watch them have sex at the same time live. I know I would have been hooked on that.

In 1993 I was going to change jobs again. You see, in 1991 I passed my mortgage broker's exam and started doing mortgages part time. By 1993 I had developed such a following that I was able to go into mortgages full time. So off I went into the wonderful world of high finance and once again, I had a job that allowed me to drive around town at my leisure. It made it possible to frequent bookstores, get high, and just plain dive head first into the pools of lies and deceit.

Because there were no restrictions on me regarding the use of drugs, it was open season for my sex addiction. Although I didn't acknowledge I was a sex addict back then, you get the point. What was going on was that since I was still smoking my feminine cigarettes, this was the thread that would tie me into my addiction. In my male mindset, I never smoked. But in my transvestite/female mindset, I always smoked. So something as insignificant as smoking became the key that would unlock the

Pandora's Box of my addiction. This is called a trigger. In re-covery I learned about this and how it was the most destructive trigger in my world. As it turned out, just smelling the smoke from a cigarette can remind me of my past. I tried looking at what brought smoking into my life, and the only thing I can think of is that I always associated with this sexy seductiveness that a woman possesses enabling her to control a male. I know that sounds a little far-fetched, but follow my thinking for a minute. You have this sexy, seductive woman dressed in high heels, a miniskirt, and great-looking make-up, and she decides to smoke. Most men drop everything just to give her a light if she's at a club. Next she controls the time by smoking slowly or quickly. If you are looking to get a little closer to her, she could say, "Wait until I finish my cigarette." It's control. Most guys will stand and wait for their princess to finish before they make another move. I think you can see my point. This is where I picked up smoking, from this attitude that a woman smoking can control a man.

Another thought that comes to mind is a memory while I was very young, five or six. My dad was driving down the Jersey Shore, and he picked up this little hottie who was smoking and he gave her a lift into Atlantic City. I was told not to tell my mother. It was our secret. I guess this was where I equated smoking with sexy women. My first vision of a leggy mini-skirted smoking girl.

Additionally, I think in general I was a controlling person. Everything had to be my way. These are the selfish views of a self-centered individual who believes the world revolves around him. I think if you looked up "self-centered" in the dictionary, you would have found my picture. I'm sure I alienated myself from lots of people just because of that behavior alone. I know this is all personal insight; however, the truth is the truth. I just think about all the times I got mad at my wife while she would drive the car. I would say things like, "You're not going fast enough" and "Move to the other lane." You get my point. This I know had led to fights more times than I want to count. Today because of my relationship with God and recovery, I just sit in the car and look out the window and enjoy the view. Whatever she does driving is what she does driving. I gave up control. I control nothing.

But back in the early 1990s, I was under the delusion that I controlled my addiction; it didn't control me. I went for a sober period of about eighteen months. I remember the incident. I had this friend who I knew for a long time—since 1987, to be exact. I used to go over her house and help her with house projects. On one particular visit, I steered the conversation to mortgages. While talking, she pulled out some pot and asked me if I'd like to get high. I said, "Sure." All I had to do was keep it a secret that I was getting high. So we continued with our mortgage conversation as I started to get high. I started to feel funny. I started to transform into my transvestite persona. My friend didn't have any idea. I got scared and abruptly told her I had to leave. I hadn't been high in over three years, so my condition was a little nerve-rattling. I became so horny. I started to fantasize about the transsexual movies I used to see. Now I was high and I couldn't go home, so I went east to the only place I knew I could be alone: to the adult bookstore. My abstinence was broken. I got the mortgage from this friend; however, I opened up Pandora's Box and it hit me with a vengeance. Once again I started spending time at the bookstores. The difference was that I started to want to interact with people. I was very nervous. I couldn't believe I had progressed to this level.

By this time, in 1994, I was doing okay at work. I was spending probably sixty-plus hours a week at the job. This was because I had to make up for the time I was spending at the bookstores and elsewhere to indulge my addiction. I had started a new habit. I would stop off at hotels and go into their bathrooms and smoke and masturbate. Of course, this was when smoking was still allowed in hotels. So here I was, driving to see clients, stopping at hotels and bookstores, smoking and masturbating two to three times a day. It was nuts. It seemed like I never had enough time to get my work done. Go figure. Unfortunately, my work suffered and I went from making six to seven thousand a month to making less than one thousand dollars a month in a very short period. I spoke to my manager and blamed my financial situation on the time of year and that the industry was slow all around. Of course, I never said I was at cause for my financial demise. Even my wife couldn't figure out why I was making so little, and

I always had to lie to cover up my activities. In April 1994, I left my company to go work for a wholesale mortgage-lending firm. I was an account representative on the street. I worked a mile from my home. My territory, however, was my whole county. I frequented the bookstores less due to my lack of funds. I made up for it with frequenting the hotels more until I started to get paranoid that people knew my M.O. In July of that same year, I was asked to come off the streets and come in house to become an assistant manager of our branch. I was relieved in that I was given a desk job, but I realized my wings were clipped so I couldn't fly to my old haunts during the day. I went into withdrawal for a period. I became very agitated and short with my wife and started to stay late at the office once again in order to masturbate in the bathroom. I even would smoke at the office when everyone went home. I was a mess.

There was an upside to this situation. Since I was brought into the office, I was forced to focus on my work, which I learned to do well. I stayed at this position until March 1996. My manager was forced to talk to me regarding my conduct at the recently past industry convention. He said I was too friendly with our clients. Now where would he get an idea like that from? The fact that I kissed every one of my female clients on the cheek and got hugs from them might have tipped him off. I was a "friendly" guy, or so I thought. Well, the regional manager was also at this convention and witnessed my activities. He was the one who addressed this issue with my manager and told him to talk to me. As far as I was concerned, my manager could go to hell with his conversation, and I told him so as well. I literally told him to "go fuck himself," and I quit right then and there. What nerve, I thought. I got on my self-righteous, selfish high horse and thought, what kind of asshole would say such a thing? I became incensed. Today I feel differently about this issue and my conduct. First of all, recovery has taught me about boundaries. At that time, I had no boundaries and each female client equated to an opportunity of pleasure, my addictive mind would say to me.

For the umpteenth time, I was once again unemployed. This caused stress to my marriage, and I would self-medicate with smoking and masturbating. Now before I got a new job, I took a week off. Each day started out the same way. My wife would get up and drive to work in North Miami. As soon as she kissed me goodbye and I smelled her scent of perfume, I would go to the bathroom and paint my lips. I would go to the laundry room and take out my hand bag, which I kept in a secret hiding place. Then I would go outside in my backyard. We had a seven-foot privacy fence and a deep thick hedge on the back side. It wasn't uncommon for me to get dressed in a pair of five-inch heels and a pair of jeans for the effect. We also had a beautiful teak patio set, where I would always sit. I would take out my cigarettes from my handbag very delicately, like a woman would pull out a long white slim cigarette from its box. I'd place it into my pursed lips and light it, taking a deep first drag. By this time, I would generally start having an erection. If not, all I had to do was dig a little deeper into my fantasy mind, which at this point was overflowing. I almost always fantasized about being a transsexual prostitute who was cruising in the adult bookstores, stopping at every booth and servicing anyone and everyone. This fantasy would get me so aroused that by the time I had finished my first cigarette, I would masturbate to full orgasm. This went on all week until I started working full time back in the cabling business. However, it laid the groundwork for future episodes of the same activity, which blossomed into a daily event for the last five years of my addiction. This occurred sometimes two or three times in a day. Now you wouldn't think I had a problem just by looking at me, but things were escalating, bringing me close to my final demise at a rapid rate.

There fortunately was a job waiting for me back in the cabling business doing commercial installation of digital music satellite antennas. I worked hard until I separated my shoulder in 1998. I tried doing the right thing by staying focused on my work. But I worked alone once again, and it became too easy to just veer off track to fulfill my urges to satisfy myself at either a bookstore or hotel. In addition to the acting out at the bookstores and hotels, I still engaged in watching transsexual videos with my wife in order to climax. I just thought she was into them as much as I was. I found out the truth later when I got into recovery. I was obsessed one particular night. I was in such turmoil inside, so much so that I found a contact to score some cocaine. I forget who it was. All I remember is that I went straight to the bookstore and stayed out until 1:00 A.M. and didn't take any pages from my wife. This would be one episode in a struggle that seemed to occur cyclically about every six months from the first episode. I finally called her crying. I was so shameful of my actions and felt guilt enough to beg for forgiveness as the tears rolled down my face. She told me to come home.

After I came home, I said to my wife as I was smoking a cigarette that I thought we needed to separate because I was bisexual and wanted to live as a woman and have sex with men. You can imagine the horror my wife felt at that time. I was still high. I was out of my mind. The drugs had saturated my brain. So anything I had said was so drug influenced. I thought she was being a prude and just didn't understand me. She said I needed to seek professional help if our marriage was to survive. This occurred in February or March of 1997. So off I went to find professional help. I found it through a rabbi and his men's group, which I met with weekly for close to a year. He was the one who suggested I go to the SAA meetings originally. After our first hour session together, I was committed to continue for the month. I didn't know what to expect. I wasn't very talkative, as a matter of record; I did very little talking. I was very angry. As far as I was concerned, my misery was caused by my wife, who didn't understand me; my parents, who fucked up raising me; and stresses from life in general. I played it off that I was just fine, all a lie of course.

It was my wife who got me to the sessions. My feelings were so closed off. I blamed my wife for all the issues. I told myself that she knew what she was getting into when she married me. So what if I did a little coke or wanted to smoke some pot? This was who I was. She either had to deal with it or find someone new. I was a real ass. I was so cold to her at home. I thought I was punishing her. The only one who was getting punished was me. I was so short-sighted. When I think of the lack of concern for my own welfare as well as the unspeakable way I treated my wife, the shame and guilt makes me shudder. Today even as I write these words, I remember the pain I put her though. Pain I never want to forget. By the grace of God, I hope and pray, one day at a time,

I never do. I thank Him at the end of each day for the support I get from Him. For His love for His guidance for His light.

Unfortunately, all this wisdom I have today is only from February 25, 2005. My past I had to pass through in order to get to my recovery. Then one of the most heartfelt hits to my emotional frame came in January 1999. I was literarily snapped into reality when my wife was diagnosed with breast cancer. My mind went into a tizzy. I was numb. I didn't know what to say. All of a sudden, the part about playing a husband had drifted away and being a husband had shown up. I can't answer how or why this shift occurred in me, but I do know it did. It was as if a light switch went on in my soul. I would flip back and forth from my addiction. One moment I was being a caring, doting husband, and then I would be off to the bookstore or in a lavatory somewhere, masturbating because the stress of the moment was upon me. Even if I didn't want to masturbate, I would find myself saying, "Why not?" I didn't have any idea what was going to happen to my wife. She was going through chemotherapy, which was so barbaric to start with, and there was nothing I could do to assist her. I felt emasculated. What good was I? So I would turn to my persona, my transvestite self, to make all the unsettling feelings disappear.

The funny part came on my wife's fourth day of her first chemotherapy treatment. My wife, who is anti-drugs and always has been, was having serious nausea episodes due to the poison in her body. I called a friend, an oncologist who lives in California, and relayed to him my wife's condition, and he recommended that I get her some marijuana right away to relieve her. She would get red like she had sunburn and she started to lose her hair after the first dose. After the first ten days from her first treatment, all her hair had come out. I was there when it first started. Neither one of us was prepared for complete baldness of her head and body. I found it very sexy. Lainie's thoughts about it were much different. She felt that the hair represented the beauty of a woman. All she had to distinguish from a man was her mane of blonde wavy locks.

But with the pot, I was clicking my heels. I was finally going to be able to get high with my wife. Again, it was all about me.

Not about relieving my wife's nausea, but me being able to smoke with her. Ha! I had finally won her over. The truth was that she did use the pot and it did relieve her symptoms immediately. The unfortunate part was that she disliked the smell of the pot more than the nausea made her feel bad. But I was able to still smoke, or so I thought.

After a few days, we got into a big argument over the pot, and her thoughts were that if I loved her I wouldn't smoke it. She wasn't going to anymore. So once again, I went into hiding with a secret life and lies about smoking pot. The part of playing a husband reared its ugly head once again. The best was when she washed my clothes and a bag of pot got washed and when I was confronted with it, I claimed I never saw it before. So as an addict, I did what comes naturally: I lied. Of course, she knew I was lying. No matter how insignificant the question was or what it was regarding, it became a way of life to lie. I really despised this way of life and no matter how hard I tried I seemed to continue doing it as long as I was in addiction.

At this time, I was working sixty to seventy hours a week. My wife needed my support, and I wanted more than anything to be there for her. I called my bosses of the two jobs I was working at the time. One was the commercial cabling I did installing the digital music for hotels, restaurants, and the like, and the second job was back in mortgage industry. This time I sold money for the commercial clients. I had worked hard in both positions, and even though it seemed like I had no time to waste, I created the extra hours I had to work because of my acting out. Emotionally I was a mess, even though I was earning about $100,000 that year. My wife was sick going through chemo. I had to make changes. A part of me came out that wasn't full of my addiction. For the first time in my life, I started thinking unselfishly. There was this human part, a part that wanted so badly to give up the money, the drugs, and the porn to take care of my wife. All at once, I made an impulsive decision to quit both jobs and go to work for Home Depot. I started working at nights. It gave me time to go to her doctor's appointments with her and to her chemo treatments. I had a regular forty-hour-work week again, but it was with flexible hours. I started to feel like a husband should be: loving, supportive, and helpful. There was only the element of my smoking feminine cigarettes with lip color that kept me connected to my addiction at that time. The thought of watching videos, getting high, or having sex with my wife under the conditions she was in was the furthest thought from my head. I was in some ways relieved. I could masturbate in the morning and night and she was not forced to participate. I thought I was doing her a favor by not pushing sex on her. Besides, I could handle myself if I got the urge. I didn't think my smoking while masturbating was a problem even if my fantasies were about wanting to be a she-male prostitute. As time passed on, my wife's chemo treatments came to an end.

Soon after all of the medications had been administered, I tried to be the best I could be. But a part of me was so rebellious. No matter how hard I tried to stop smoking and masturbating in the mornings after my wife would go to work, I failed. The impulse to act out was stronger then I was capable of controlling. It was as if there was an inner control that lived inside me. It made me very confused. I felt less than as a man and decided to go back to the internet to try and fulfill my manliness, meeting a new woman who liked my fetish and who understood me. I was complete if I was in a relationship with a woman who could partner up with my fetishes, a sad commentary for a guy who couldn't distinguish between reality and fantasy. Months ago, I was a doting husband. Now I was resenting my wife because she didn't understand me.

It is said that if you ever want to find anything you can imagine, the internet can provide it for you. It's true. By 2000 my wife was back to work and I was happily entrenched in internet porn. I found a website that was for alternate lifestyles, a place I thought I fit. I created a profile that I felt described me to a tee:

Married bisexual male transvestite smoker looking to serve and party with.
Looking for female to engage with.
Wife doesn't understand me."

As I said in the beginning chapter, the quote "doesn't understand me" would thread through my life. Funny how I felt no one ever understood me. I was always ready to point the finger at everyone else instead of trying to figure out myself first. This profile was the bait to find my new partner, the one, the only partner who would finally understand me. Regardless if my wife was in the next room, I was on the website checking my mail—checking for that special someone who was as depraved as I was. I became more daring; sometimes I would check my mail when my wife was five feet from me in the kitchen. I didn't care. I had progressed so far in my addiction since I started on the net, it was scary. Since my days off were in the middle of the week, when my wife was working, I would dress up on those days and sit outside on the patio and fantasize for hours at a time, smoking and masturbating until I was bloody. Then at night when my wife got home, I would become very agitated and yell at her for the smallest of reasons. I was unbearable. We had very little physical contact. There was no intimacy to speak of. The longer the time between actual physical contact, the more agitated I would become, not recognizing that the two were tied together. Then I would go act out again and again to soothe my savage soul. I felt I deserved to get myself off. I owed it to myself to take care of me since my wife wasn't interested in me. Such convoluted thoughts ran through my mind day in and day out. I was isolating myself so badly that even though my wife and I slept in the same bed, I felt so alone that no one could reach me.

This type of activity took me away for hours at a time. I could sit there at the desk and get into a chat room and lose track of all time, to the point that the dawn would be coming and I still hadn't gone to sleep. My wife would still be sleeping and had no idea I was still up. The only saving grace I had was that I didn't have to be to work until nine o'clock most days. I felt so alone from these activities after I would get offline that the only way to combat the loss was to go back online. It was such a vicious cycle, and I was powerless against it.

Things got back in control, or so I thought, when I started to work days again in late 2000. I was getting up at four-thirty in the morning to be at a teaching position I was chosen for by the main

Home Depot headquarters in Atlanta. I was one of eight in the southeastern part of the United States to train associates as part of a new sales program. It was a great opportunity. In fact, I met one of my closest friends from this group. I was so busy with the curriculum that I really didn't have much time for anything else. The job with Home Depot lasted until May 2003. I left due to differences in management ideas and styles and opened a custom closet company. It gave me freedom once again. I continued my smoking and watching the transsexual videos at home with my wife when we did engage in sex. I still felt empty. Especially since I would masturbate while I smoked, so the feelings of shame ran deep like waters in a hidden cave. The guilt kept piling up day by day until I snapped again and confronted my wife with the insight suggesting I was bisexual or gay. I just couldn't shake this monkey off my back. I knew down deep inside I was broken and I needed to be cast aside like bad trash. I kept asking my wife why she would stay with such a loser. We would cry together, and then she would say that if I was gay I wouldn't want to have sex with her. She wasn't wrong. I was so confused and delusional during these times that it seemed better that I not be in relationship with her. Everything would be smoothed over for a while until my next episode, the worst of which happened in November 2004, a month after my father's death. My father's death was the straw that broke the camel's back for me emotionally and psychologically. It happened very suddenly.

After he died, I felt like the lowest, most valueless person on the planet. I had just spoken to my father on the day before he died, Sunday, October 17, 2004, around 8:30 P.M. I called him because my wife's ex-mother-in-law had passed away that evening. I felt extremely sad, and it made me reflect on my relationship with my dad. Because of my difficult relationship with my mother, I wasn't able to see my dad very often, so we had kept in contact over the phone. He was my unofficial business consultant. He was proud of what I was doing and even told me so. Well, I called him and asked him to please contact me if he ever got sick and wasn't able to see me so I could go to him regardless of my mom. I told him I loved him very much and wanted the opportunity to be able to care for him. He just blew it off by saying he was fine and not to worry. He told me he loved me, and I said the same to him and we hung up. The next day, Monday, October 18, 2004, he died of a heart attack. I wasn't notified. My parents lived two and half miles from me. Tuesday of that week, I called him and got no answer on his cell phone service. I called back Wednesday and got no answer again. I called my aunt, my mother's sister, and I got no answer there. I was getting nervous. I mentioned to my wife my concerns. She told me not to worry, that I'd probably reach him on the next day. Thursday came. I tried calling countless times with no answers. I was extremely nervous by this time. This was a person I spoke to almost every day for close to a year and now nothing, my aunt too, nothing. I had a very restless evening that night when I went to bed. Then Friday came and I had a scheduled installation job to do in Coconut Grove. I was in transit with an employee of mine who knew what I was going through regarding my dad, and she suggested that I call the police and have them check it out. I did just that. An hour later, I got a phone call from the police, who told me a neighbor of my parents wanted to talk to me and would call me in a minute. The neighbor did. He was sorry to inform me that my father had passed away on Monday, four days earlier, and my mother had taken his body up to Pennsylvania and buried him. When I asked why I wasn't notified, he said he asked my mother if he should notify me and she told him that he wasn't to call me and let me know. She didn't want me to know he had died. This was my dad, the man who raised me and showed me love as he could. He cared for me. He told me he loved me four days earlier. What right did she have to take my right away from me to say goodbye to him? She didn't care. Now that my father was gone, she didn't have to worry what he thought. It was her way of saying, "Fuck you," to me. "You're not my son, and now you're out of my life completely." That was the coldest most inhuman way to treat another human being I have ever known.

This is what broke me emotionally. I began acting out on a daily basis again to take away the pain. I didn't even get a chance to grieve his death. I just kept acting out to numb the pain. One parent died, and one kicked me to the curb. I didn't have anything to live for. The one person in my life who loved me unconditionally was gone. You see, I had a bond with him that I hadn't had with any other person, including my wife, so as far as I was concerned, I was totally alone. I was spiritually bankrupt, psychologically a wreck, and emotionally shot. I was in a downward spiral, and all I could think of was soothing myself. I couldn't get the pain to go away and wasn't able to grieve, and I had a tremendous amount of shame and guilt. I was a mess. I found a contact for cocaine and on that Friday night, right before going out with friends, I just vanished. I didn't care about anything or anyone. All I thought in my mind was, *Let's get coke and become the best transsexual prostitute in the world. Fuck everyone else.*

I went straight to the adult bookstore. I remember it like it was yesterday. I didn't want to go, really. There was something inside me that kept saying, "Fuck everyone. Go, go, get high and fly. You know you are really a transsexual bitch just waiting to start hooking. You need to go watch the girls in the movies so you can learn how to become a better slut. You're a coke whore and this is your life. Fuck everyone else."

This was playing in my head, that inner voice. I went with it. I was so angry inside. When I finally got to the bookstore, I had cigarettes, coke, lip color, and a compact. I was ready to get down. I had to be the best. I had to see the lip print on my cigarette. I had to smoke the whole pack because I was a whore and all good whores smoked at least a pack a day. I even took my phone in with me and listened to it ring over and over again as my wife kept trying to reach me as the hours kept slipping by. I was paralyzed in the state I was in. I couldn't move. I could not get up. I was in such a drug-induced delusional state, I couldn't leave. I was all twisted up. My head was swirling. I didn't go home until five o'clock the next morning. When I ran out of drugs, I started to come down and crash with such shame and guilt, all I could think of was dying. I didn't want to live. Once again I had torn my wife's heart out and ripped our relationship to shreds. She didn't want me in the house. I cried. I bawled like a baby. I couldn't understand how I could have hurt her again. I was a piece of shit. I felt like the lowest piece of life form. I wasn't worthy to live or have a relationship. I had a 9-mm gun in my possession and wanted so badly to swallow the barrel. I couldn't, though, because all I could think about was that my wife would have to clean up the mess. I was out of control. I was in so much emotional pain, I just wanted to die and be with my father. I missed him so much.

The last acting-out episode prompted my wife to give me an ultimatum: If I didn't seek professional mental health care, I was out of the marriage. This wasn't an option. It just happened that I met a therapist at Home Depot when I worked there back in 2003. I had her card. I called her and broke down over the first phone call to her. I made an appointment and saw her the next day. Caren was excellent: compassionate, loving, and encouraging. She allowed me to open up, since I never had before. It was a breath of fresh air. I was in so much pain I was ready to give therapy a chance. I didn't want to live this way any longer. I was always tired. I was sleeping every moment I had. I was tired of being tired of being tired. I had had it. So the journey of discovering who I am officially began. Not that I was aware of it at the time; Caren really had a way with me. She got me to open up. We talked about my childhood, my mother, my father's death, and my mother's actions handling my father's death. I fell short discussing my sex addiction. In my mind, I didn't have a sex addiction. I wasn't a sex addict. Every time she would recommend that I consider going to a men's group where sex addiction was discussed, I would say, "I'm not going."

It was December 2004 at this time, and I was still acting out even though my wife was threatening divorce. Nothing seemed to make me feel better. As far as I was concerned, my wife was still the issue, not me. I wanted out of the marriage. My wife just didn't understand me. I wanted to swing, get high, dress up, and live care free. I must have married the wrong person, so I thought. My head was swimming with fantasy, delusions of what life would be like without her. The grass was greener on the other side, and I wanted a fresh start. I thought if I was away from my wife, it would stop all the pain.

I expressed this feeling to Caren and told her I needed to move out. I needed to be a free man to live the life I was meant.

Not a life that I felt my wife "trapped" me into living. Caren supported my moving out. I don't think she liked the idea. My addiction was loving this. I was so close to living free. Sex, drugs, and rock-n'-roll, here I come. FTW: "Fuck the world," my mind was saying. My heart was in so much pain. My life was totally out of control. Leaving seemed to be the right answer. I was so confused about which way to turn. On one hand, I had the life I lived with my wife for fifteen years, and on the other hand was a chance for freedom, so I thought. Caren suggested if I was going to leave that I should speak to my wife face to face and let her know how I felt. I couldn't do that. I couldn't even write it down. I took me until the new year to get the nerve to write down my thoughts. I sat at the computer that I used for all my liaisons and wrote the most difficult letter of my life....

January 5, 2005

Before you get upset, please know that writing this letter is probably one of the hardest things I've ever undertaken in my life. Caren also wanted to let you know she is available for you if you need to speak to her.

With that being said, it has come to pass that I need to separate myself from the one thing that I question the most: our relationship. I'm not asking to divorce. I'm looking to get clarity of what we have and what my needs are for both of us. Without this I'm afraid our relationship will flounder endlessly in a pool of uncertainty. Please understand, I have tried for days to write this letter to you. I have become sick to my stomach to leave the one person and relationship I have had for the longest time. This separation is not meant to harm you, rather strengthen us if there is to be an us.

With my much love and pain,
Your Jakey

I handed the letter to Lainie and started to cry. She wasn't crying. I think she felt relief that the burden of her pain was now leaving. I remember that night so well, I even wrote about it in my journal. I took some clothes and put them into a bag and left the house. I drove to the hotel down the road and checked in. I decided to record my thoughts and feelings on my laptop for future reference. Here is my first entry:

January 5, 2005

It's 9:59 P.M., and I'm all alone in a hotel room. I've called my therapist on her pager and left the hotel phone number with the room number. I hope she calls it.

I did what I'm supposed to do. I wrote my wife a letter explaining how I feel and gave it to her at 6:30 P.M.. I had tears in my eyes as she started to read it, and she gave me a hug as I started to cry knowing I was leaving a few minutes later.

I'm on my own again. I haven't been on my own since I left my first wife fifteen years ago to live with strangers. It's scary out here alone. So many different feelings are going through my head.

The phone just rang in my room. It was Caren, my therapist. She got my page. She can't talk now. She will call me back later on tonight after her class is over.

What am I doing? Where do I go from here? For the last fifteen years, I've felt that I have been living a lie about who I am. Who people see. Who I share my feelings with. There are some people who I say know me. After looking back on the last fifteen years, I say these people only know who I let them see who I created as the person I call me, not who I am. If I am sum of all my parts. Then I am what my experiences have created. I question this. This is why I am alone right now. To review who I am. To get clarity of my sexuality. To get clarity of what my boundaries will become.

I guess to understand where I am now, I should go back to where I've been. This will be where I start to unravel the intricate life I've lived with and struggled to find peace with. I hope writing this helps others who have gone through or lived with struggles similar to mine. Strangely, I find solitude in putting these sentences to print. I hope my own healing acts as a blanket of warmth to those who know someone or love someone who has gone through or is going through times like mine. God bless you.

I'm tired. I'm going to bed. It's 11:50 P.M.. This hotel room isn't warm. It doesn't smell like home. I miss home.

As you can see, there were a lot of feelings, but I felt no emotions. I was void of showing any emotions at that time. I was deep in my addiction. That night I "celebrated" my freedom by going to the video store around the corner before I started writing and rented two porn DVDs. I stayed up until midnight after rubbing myself raw from masturbating. I was so confused at this time. I was sad that my marriage seemed to be falling apart at the seams, and I was alone like I always wanted to be so I could pursue my life's ambitions of being a transsexual prostitute. My wife was finally out of the picture. I could do as I chose. So why was I so sad? I was perplexed by these conflicting emotions.

The next day, I awoke to the smell of stale cigarettes and that damp musty smell of cheap motel rooms. I was sad again. I called a friend of mine whose house I was going to be staying. Kari was home and told me come down when I was ready. When my wife asked me where I was going to live, I told her about this friend of mine who was female and I had mentioned her name before. She told me if I was going to a female's house that the relationship we had was definitely over. So I did what any addict would do, I lied to my wife once again. I told her my friend was a lesbian.

When I got to Kari's house, it was a serene location. It was off the New River in an old historic area. The four-apartment complex had ample room in each of its apartments for two people. The complex was on the river, so the peaceful language of the water would speak to me when I sat quietly reading a book. I did that quite often. My friend was pretty accommodating. I had my own bedroom with my own bathroom. There were lots of candles that burned regularly, keeping the air in the apartment smelling spicy but not overpowering. She had a dog as well. Max was a Catahoula Leopard Hound, a very special breed that is a fearless and tireless companion. Max had one blue eye and one brown eye and reminded me of a calico cat with four colors. He was very rambunctious when it came time for a walk but listened well to commands. Max became a good friend and good listener, although he didn't really give his opinion back to me. This made him the perfect friend.

This woman friend was into metaphysical spiritual thinking. She was a mosaic artist, and I met her while I was at Home Depot. She became a customer whenever she was looking for new colors for her newest projects. She did terrific pieces. She was so gifted. She told me to feel comfortable in the house and use all of the appliances at my leisure. She was a friend. I knew her for four years before I called her in a panic one day and asked her if I could move into her open second bedroom. She knew my story; I had opened up to her before moving into her home. There's a comfort I've always had with artists who make me feel comfortable letting out my feelings or showing a glimpse of who I really was or in reality a glimpse of who I thought I really was. It was all so confusing. In any case, Kari had a glimmer of who I was claiming to be. I just remember that I was physically so tired and my mind was working overtime and I had trouble slowing down my thoughts when I tried going to bed. Thank God for Tylenol PM; it helped me with my headaches and sleep issues in the beginning as I was getting acclimated to my new surroundings. What really helped me was being alone. Even though I lived in the same house as Kari, we were only roommates. We weren't buddy-buddy. She lived her life with her friends, and I isolated myself for the most part except to work out and go to work. On January 15, I made a new entry into my journal.

January 15, 2005
5:03 A.M.

I miss the kids. I just woke to the realization, the kids I miss. This is painful. I miss the look in her eyes when she greets me at the door. The look of desire.

As I know tomorrow is today. I stretch knowing this too shall pass. How long I'll be attached to the pain, I can't say. I'll see and watch.

Goodnight for now.

I was still really in denial of my feelings. On this day, I was reminiscing about how my wife made me feel as she greeted me at the door. But I pushed down those feelings because I felt I was on a mission. I was so into my addiction that I started back on the computer on AOL. It had been like I wasn't away for years. The moment I joined back on, I was like a fish to water. I just swam into the direction of depravity. I was alone. I was my own man even though I was acting like such a selfish child, saying, "I want, I want, I want." I want to get high. I want to do nothing. I want to smoke. I want to act out on the computer. I want, I want, I want—like a two year-old. I had a rude awakening on the fifteenth. I ran out of clean clothes. I also ran out of food at the apartment. The food didn't bother me as much. I just started eating out a lot. The clothes, however, were a different story. I hadn't done laundry since I'd left my wife. I needed to think quickly. I needed to make my life easier. I gathered all of my clothes, threw them into my work van, and drove to the Laundromat down the street from the apartment. Next I had to conquer the food issue. So I devised an idea. I proposed to Kari if she would pick up my food, I would pay her for her time as a personal shopper. God knows I was making money hand over fist at the time. In one hand, out through the fingers on the other hand. She agreed. So there I was, a little spoiled brat getting others to do for me so I could have more time to act out.

January 16, 2005
6:02 A.M.

I just awoke to the thought that I'm out of control. I'm not watching what I'm eating, I'm not working out properly. I'm not doing 1 on 1's with BNI, I'm out of control. I also noticed how easily I'm able to crush down my true feeling through avoidance.

I'm tired of thinking. I'm visually watching the presence of life unfold minute by minute. Conscious to the earth's calling for PEACE. I watched as an opportunity to further the next step of a project showed up. It unfolded like a table napkin gracefully opening after a soft roll.

The step I am speaking about is in the Peace Park Project. I am looking for an artist rendering of the complex, nothing elaborate. Just a drawing showing the buildings.

I have the vision so deeply engrained, I could pull it out with forceps. What's even funnier is through this process tonight, I gained the knowledge I needed to further move ahead. So tomorrow I'll stop and get as many names of companies with real estate signs showing complex renderings and call them up and find out who does their signs and call that company. Ask them all who want to donate their time and go down in history as the company that backed the company that backed the conceptual designer who created the art that shifted the consciousness of the planet.

Nothing like a grandiose project to keep my focus away from my issues. I was full of ideas. The problem was I wouldn't finish what I started except for the jobs for which I was getting paid. However, when it came to finish projects in my house, I would get about 90 percent complete and then because I was almost done with the project, I would reward myself with acting out. So the cycle would be endless and the wreckage of projects not completed lay in my path.

January 17, 2005

It's 1:30PM. I decided to write down my activities as they are so that you can see me, as I am doing everything I'm doing so you can better evaluate me. I do not want to hide anything. I just got done getting high on pot. I smoked. After that I felt a change in my personality. I was becoming effeminate, hot, and horny. I wanted a cigarette. I went back to my room and got my purse and went out back of the apartment, sat down on a stoup, and opened my purse, grab my box of feminine cigarettes, and pulled one out and lit it. I wanted to feel relaxed, so I went back into my purse to get a tube of mauve lipstick. I wanted to see the female imprint. At this point it's all about me feeling good, looking hot, and feeling sexy as well. I'm feeling very bitchy, smutty, and I am confused as to the validity of my posi-

tion. On one hand, I'm totally into wanting to become a girl like those I watch in my videos, feeling it's where I need to be in my life, a transsexual prostitute. Exactly like the videos titles are.

On the other hand, I feel lost. Not able to make rational decisions other than wanting to get high, smoking, and having sex. Notice I say that these are what I'm considering to be rational choices. I'm not sure this is the right way to be for me. I know it feels good. I feel right for me in a weird kind way. Am I stuck in a dimension that is a vehicle for my success? Or am in a fantasy that I'm portraying as reality? Either way I'm not sure. All I know is I'm just being with it all.

I did two design appointments today equaling ten closets. I have the information and will start the process of designing them later today. My head is swimming now, running rampant with idea after idea. I do not sense the ability to concentrate to long before I flitter to a new idea. I haven't put together the appointment with a M.D. regarding medication. It's suggested I do so. I'm fallen asleep.

On this day, I was feeling lost, alone in my isolation. You could hear the delusion as clear as music on a radio. The confusion of realities really hits me hard as I reread this passage. I had no self-esteem as I aspired to become a transsexual prostitute. My thoughts were only on getting high and smoking and thinking about acting out. From this vantage point, it's sad to see the depth that I thought was the epitome of life. I felt so lousy after I smoked. I know I wanted to but afterwards, I was saddened that I did. My mind would race and after I came down, I was full of shame, guilt, and confusion. This was the time that I went back to my computer and started really looking for the "perfect partner."

I had an idea of what I was looking for. I wanted a dominant female who had a smoking fetish and wanted her partner to be a transvestite and really got turned on by me prostituting myself and do XXX videos for her financial gains. You really have to watch what you ask for because you may end up getting it.

I forget the woman's name, but she ran a website I had found. It was a smoking-fetish website. She was the webmaster and it was geared towards amateurs; these women were not professionals in the sex trade business. On the contrary, the women who worked on this site were your neighbor next door, single moms, college girls, married professional women who all had a fetish to live out their smoking fetish dreams engaging in sex while smoking and being videotaped. They were straight, bi, lesbian, and every look you could imagine with the common denominator being they all had a smoking fetish. So I contacted the website and asked to speak to the webmaster. I emailed her and told her how much I liked her website and how cool I thought it would be to work for her. Now just to let you know everyone "worked" for free. They did it just for the kicks. She responded that she was very intrigued with what I wrote and requested I follow up with another email, which I did immediately. I was so excited by what was going on that I had started to intensely fantasize about our meeting someday. I remember rubbing myself raw on more than one day over this intrigue.

It finally came to a head, and she asked to speak with me over the phone. I dropped everything I was doing and made myself available to her call. I remember the first call. We seemed to connect in a very depraved way. She loved the idea of me serving her and even liked the possibility of me training her current male slave how to better serve men. I was so immersed in this fantasy that I told her I wanted to do a video myself so she could financially gain from it. I was willing to serve her needs by prostituting myself for her gain. All she had to do was make sure I had the drugs I needed. This is a woman who currently has her daughter and daughter-in-law working for her in smoking fetish videos. She even has fetish parties where twenty-five to thirty guys are invited who like smoking fetish girls so they can have sex. She told me that at the last party she personally satisfied each guy to completion while she smoked. I was so excited; finally I had found the woman of my dreams. She liked the idea of having a transvestite as a slave for herself so much so that we started to plan a personal meeting. I was enamored. I really thought that I had found nirvana. We also talked about the type of video I would do for her.

I wanted to do a gang bang with five guys. She loved it. She knew she could find the guys and knew where to get me the drugs I needed. She supported my whole fantasy and looked forward to me making money for her. I was living in the bowels of hell. My partner was the devil herself who supported my depravity.

Where was my head? We set a date to meet in first week of March 2005. I started looking for airline tickets to fly up to Newark Airport. She lived ten minutes away from the airport. What was I doing? What had my life been reduced to? Before, in late 2004, I had spoken to my life insurance agent and secured a policy for seven hundred fifty thousand dollars. My wife was the sole beneficiary. What I realized I was doing became very clear to me after I was in recovery. I was covertly setting up my suicide. This was no joke. If I had gone to meet this "perfect" match of mine and played out my fantasy of being a transvestite prostitute engaging in a porn video of me doing a gang bang, that would have been the coffin. The shame I would have felt and guilt I would have gone through would have been the lid. Somehow I would have ended up dead. Whether it was "accidentally" falling out a window or blowing out my heart on an overdose from cocaine or meth, it would have happened. There was no returning back to my Lainie. I would have sunk to the lowest of lows. I would have been marked, scarred, and never would have returned to life.

January 18, 2005
11:12 A.M.

I worked out, 8 A.M. Tough day knowing what I've missed and how I'm eating. I just went and remembered that I went back to 46th Street, made an invoice for Allied, p/u: 23 to give to Doron for safe keeping. I'll get him my 26 ASAP. After I dropped the invoice to Allied, I went to Doron's, then came back to Sailboat Bend. I couldn't wait to get back. Get high, then smoke a cigarette, then watch videos till I cum.

So I did all that. Now I'm looking at what I have to do for work. Is this okay? I question this. I know I have work to do. I know that I'm writing this. I think I'm in an okay space. I be-

lieve I have some control over my faculties. I'm not sure what. I couldn't wait to get high. I couldn't wait to get my make-up on or see my lip print on the end of cigarette knowing the intense feeling of pleasure I was going to get from my orgasm. It all sends shiver down my spine. In a good way and an odd way, now I need to work.

Here I am. Today Caren called at 3:30 P.M. "I was caught." *So to speak. I had just gotten high, smoking a very effeminate cigarette, and my neighbor was using the trash can as I was sitting there with my purse, rhinestone glasses, smoking this effeminate cigarette. It was interesting to watch the moment. I was taken back by her call; I was high and was watching how I was interacting with her while the neighbor just looked and smiled at me. Hmmm. I was nervous. I was in public, sort of. I wanted to enjoy my cigarette. I was in the "zone." All I could think about wanting to relax and get to my video training. It seems sick to think I am studying this material as if I was in a private school. My mind swirls when I think I'm so close to the edge. The edge of what? Why am I here? Am I calling out to a stream, or is this intertwined in my circuitry so deep it's the flow of normalcy for me? Or is it that my wiring can be rewired? I'm not sure I'll ever be able to get the dynamic of this equation.*

All the feelings that erupt inside me are the same since I was sixteen, almost seventeen. I can see the clear distinction of each space. I would get high, smoke only. Smoke cigarettes, and then chase the orgasm. My question is this: Is this a flow that assists in this writing, that assists in my ability to feel deeper the skin I am in? The ability to feel my muscles as they are transforming as well? Is this springboard one-sided or two? Can I be this I see? Am I already there and not going over the edge for fear? Am I already here and the way I'm living my life is acceptable? I want these questions to become clear. I feel alone. I understand there are dynamics that created the being I am today. What I need to know is, am I at the level of life that I have a choice where all the issues will peel away or am to em-

brace this life that I'm in? I'm not sure I have enough data yet. I'm petrified.

January 18, 2005
9:14 P.M.

It's continuing again, these feelings that I can touch with my mind after my orgasm or during. This light. This inner feeling of expansion. A jolt so intense, my perspective on issues adjusts even for a split second. The amount of information stored or followed at the split second of awareness of my intensity of orgasm is the most intense. Follow my mental path, harness the serge of data as it pierces into my conscious mind, and hold onto your thoughts and intertwine the two and I get an awaking of my core of me.

January 18, 2005
11:29 P.M.

I came again looking at the videos. What I saw was the direction I am focused on...the fact of having a cigarette was also a part of the prop. I'm in a group of guys all getting head, and it feels good to be touching their bodies. I'm thinking about relaxing, smoking a cigarette, and the feeling directed to my lower portion of body, more specifically my anus is twitching in pleasure on the notion future penetrations are to occur. I'm smiling, wanting the moment to continue on. This is the time I captured in that fleeting moment at the height of my orgasm. Which happened to also be incredibly intense— this brings out the question at hand. I was high, was I in the same stream I remember from earlier and years back? I am. Am I to steer clear of this recognized energy? This is the stream I've been in since I was sixteen or so. A mental consciousness about the clear interaction with nature in a curious fashion. The ability to be observant of my surroundings similar to that of a cat on the prowl at night. The clarity to see in the darkness. Is this the channel of memory that needs to be rewired? What is it about

my thoughts that I'm throwing some much drama and at-
tachment to it? I look forward to Caren on Wednesday.

As I reread these words, I am so glad I am in recovery. My thoughts seemed to be all over the place. My purpose can clearly be seen as one-dimensional. It's all wrapped around sex almost twenty-four hours a day by this point. I kept running back to my apartment, isolating myself from everyone, including my room-mate, except for my addiction. My addiction was the only conversation I was willing to have. It's like it was its own entity.

I remember myself talk how the chatter seemed to have a demonic tone. It ruled my life. I was not present too much around me, only what my mind was saying to me—like there was a little man controlling my every move. I was in a robotic state. I'd wake up in the morning, and the first thing I would do was masturbate. I would lay myself down to fall asleep at night, and I would masturbate. As I breathed every breath, so my addiction would speak in my mind. If the activity of the day didn't involve sex in some sort of manner, I would find something or someone who did. By this time, nine out of every ten phone calls were with intrigue interests or people with whom I could have phone sex. I had no time for anyone in my life if sex wasn't part of the equation. How shallow was I? All I know is the people who knew me really had no clue as to who I really was and what my activities were.

January 19, 2005
11:01 A.M.

I came back to Sailboat Bend. Today is my day, I said, so I want
to get high and watch videos, smoke, and sleep. What a waste
of energy. I see this after I've gone ahead and done the damage
of continuing my day in a committed way. Is this statement
rational? Is this the attitude of a junkie, sleaze-ball sex addict?
Am I even in reality? I feel a stream of energy running
through me. I can feel the low hum. Like an electrical charge
slowly drifting through me.

I'm agitated. I'm agitated because I'm not happy being
high right now. That's the thought right now. I'm just being

with the acceptance that if I indulge, there are consequences with which I have to live. Then right this minute I see another question—no, a statement—appeared in my mind. It says, "Is this right under the surface of what is driving me and being high uncovers the truth?" I'm on the edge again. Papa, I hope you can help me distinguish between the two. Do I have to make a choice? I have so many choices. I'm retreating again. I feel overwhelmed in one sense because instead of not getting high, I chose to be high. I'm just going to keep on writing until I'm straight again. Then I'm going to look at my feelings and write what shows up then. Evaluate the distinction, if there is one.

January 19, 2005
11:12 P.M.

I AM NOT ALONE. Okay, there, I said it. I'm not alone. There, I said it again. I hear my talk, my chatter. The truth is I isolate myself in a way and this is going to sound weird, but I'm beginning to embrace the female side of myself, like metamorphosing into something different.

I see anger on this day. It's also the first time I gave reference to myself being a sex addict. I felt like I'm out of control. What amazes me the most is that I can clearly see how I was a slave to my addiction. The insanity it took me through. This day was thirty-eight days before my divine intervention, and all I could think of was three things, "Me, me, and me." My world revolved around my bedroom, adult bookstores, and an adult theater. My day's activities consisted of being on internet porn sites while masturbating, looking at the transsexual videos while masturbating, or performing sexual acts at the adult theater with anonymous partners. This was a snapshot of my life. I let my work fall by the wayside. I would call fantasy lovers and talk for hours about my daily exploits of immoral acts. Put all these activities and combine them with smoking pot or cocaine, and you get one hell of a sex cocktail.

I'm so lucky I'm alive today. Only for the grace of God, I'm alive today. I was so scared of myself when I said I was beginning to embrace my female side. I remember at this time, in a pot-stoned stupor, fantasizing about getting breast implants. Looking in the mirror in the bathroom and having a conversation with myself about myself looking so hot in my make-up that I must be the woman inside my head I say I am. This moment scared the hell out of me. Was I actually a woman in a man's body? How do you know? These were questions I would ask myself after I came. Before I would climax, my thoughts were all screaming inside my head how I was the best-looking slut on TV and that I needed to practice my profession of prostitution. Times like this would also wind me up so much that I would abstain from climaxing and tell myself to get dressed and go to the theater and have as much oral sex as I could. Then I would grab my heels, my bag, and my clothes, contact my coke connection, and go to the theater and actually act out with as many guys as I could until I ran out of coke. I had no control. I felt like a Stepford wife, except I was a transvestite. In my mind, I was being who I thought I was meant to be, and my body followed in every aspect down to the clothes and make-up.

January 21, 2005
11:49 P.M.

I'm high. This is what showed up. I MISS MY DAD. I really do. Pop, you know I love you. I know you see me. You were the one person my heart broke for. I miss you. I didn't have anyone else. You were my only contact with the world. You see my relationship with Lainie. No one calls me. No one else ever really calls. I'm not going to apologize to you for who I am. I know that sounds odd. I'm who I am. I guess it didn't turn out right for you, either. Pop, I was so mad at how you were treated. I knew the only thing I could do was just love you. You were the best. I knew you had it hard. I know you could not leave. Look, it took a lot for me to leave Lainie. I still love her. I never knew what it would be like after you were gone. I do now. My life is on my own now. My train came in, and I have to go for that big ticket in the sky. You know, Pop. You weren't alone. I love you and miss you.

It's so clear to see how I was isolating myself. That I felt that I had no one else in the world who cared for me except my dad. I even discounted how Lainie felt for me. I know today that she is the only one with whom I need to concern myself. She truly is my best friend, my lover, my companion. I'm very blessed that she is in my life. Something else I uncovered was that I made it okay to live my life as I thought I was supposed to live it without the fear of my father being humiliated. That fact that I allowed myself to become humiliated in private and public never registered. The power of this disease twists reality into a silk-spun web of denial and delusion. I was so blind. The really scary part of this entry is where I reflect upon "having to go for that big ticket in the sky." I know I was having suicidal thoughts; however, I never thought I ever wrote anything relative to it. This passage turned out to be an eye-opening experience.

I remember being in contact with that web mistress for the smoking fetish site. I didn't care about who I was leaving, what clients I was skipping out on. I was destined to fulfill my life and if I died doing it, so what? All I wanted was more drugs, coke, meth, I didn't care. "I'm a prostitute," I kept proclaiming over and over, day in and day out, through every joint I smoked to every drag on my cigarette. I constantly kept reinforcing the negative behavior, thinking it was exactly how my life should be, never realizing the devastating effect it was having on me. Then there was the constant "nap time," where I would have to sleep for a few hours because I drained myself physically.

January 23, 2005
4:57 P.M.

I haven't written much, been feeling myself in my own skin. What does it feel like, you ask? Well, I remember how I felt when I used to get high, stretch, and work out in dance. I let myself feel that again. I have been doing it before I go to bed. I feel so relaxed and refreshed when I'm finished. It's me. It's what I do when I get high. I love to dance, alone. I dance with people ONLY if I feel like it. It's my form of release. A healthy release. I still smoke and like to dress. I'm starting to accept this, I think. I even did my own laundry. I miss Lainie. That I can't deny. I miss that sassy devilish look in her eyes. I'm thinking of sending her flowers for Valentine's Day, signed, "Happy Valentine's Day, Love, A Girlfriend." I wonder if she would get it. A question. Today is an interesting day. Today is officially ten days of separation. I acknowledge that. That's it.

I know I was getting high a lot, trying to fit a square peg in a round hole. I was always "trying" to fit into my skin. I was driving myself mad with this conversation. My life did not make me happy. I remember wanting so desperately to just "out" myself. I couldn't; it didn't seem right. Almost every gay person I ever spoke to knew they were gay at some point in their young life but may have waited until their adult life to come out. I didn't feel that way. I didn't fit in any world except the one I had secretly. There were no other people in my circle except for those people into the "lifestyle," and even they had normal lives. I wanted my "lifestyle" to be twenty-four-seven. No one was into it as much as I was. People I thought were my friends said I had a problem and I wasn't living reality. I never heard them at all. I blew them off, thinking they just didn't understand. Then on the other side of the coin, I still had desires for my wife in a pure sense. I wanted her to understand that this was me. What I see is a desperate attempt to "play" the role of husband, not be a husband. All I could do at this time was get high, smoke, and daydream or fantasize about my newfound mistress. She was my answer. She said I could do everything I wanted: smoke, prostitute myself, do drugs, and basically whore myself to her every whim. I was buying into her depravity. I had been begging women for this chance, the opportunity to humiliate myself without any regard for my own safety. To me this was my nirvana. This was the fantasy I kept replaying in my mind over and over while I was high and reinforcing with every orgasm. By this time, I was one month away from my divine intervention and the lowest point of my life had yet to come.

For the next couple of weeks, I was concentrating on setting up my new life. My friend Marc kept calling me asking how I was doing. I couldn't let him know how I felt because I didn't know how I felt. The delusion of this being my nirvana life was being replayed in my head so often that I had retreated to my bedroom to get on the net every chance I could to continue with my "education." I had to watch the transsexual videos at least twice a day or hours in the evening. I would concentrate on the characters' every move, every nuance. I had to be perfect. When it got late at night, I would put on my make-up and, in between orgasms from the video, take an unlit cigarette and practice seductive smoking in the mirror using my image as the person I was seducing. This became increasing sexual as if I had a twin and it was her I was seducing. I would take this ritual all the way to orgasm and then go back to the internet to get another fix of videos. There was no time for anyone or anything else; it was all about me. I was being probably the most narcissistic person at this time in my life, and I'm sure some people who knew me just wanted to vomit.

Then in the middle of these weeks, I got a phone call from an old "friend" with whom I would act out. This was a very volatile relationship. This was a guy I knew from my Home Depot days. He knew my desires pretty well, even my desire for drugs. He was the person who introduced me to crystal methamphetamine and the seedy world that goes with it. I was truly mesmerized with this drug and the opportunity to live like the prostitute I dreamed of becoming. He allowed me to dress and flaunt myself for his pleasure, knowing once he gave me the drugs that I would do anything for him. Crystal methamphetamine is like no other drug; it's made from household chemicals and has the potential for addiction upon its first introduction. It's truly the devil's handiwork.

I was in my glory, so I thought. Totally dressed down to five-inch heels and full make-up. Smoking my long feminine cigarettes and listening to music as he would tease me with the clear Pyrex pipe that had the crystal in it. The method he taught me was to smoke it. This is the most highly addictive way of using this drug, and I begged to become addicted to it. I wanted it. I wanted so desperately to become a street hooker. This was my ambition. I had no other thoughts in my mind. It was all about that moment we were in. I knew what I was doing. I smiled as I took each deep drag from the pipe. If he took one hit, I wanted five before I gave it back. He egged me on. He started saying how hot I was and how much I turned him on. This sent me into a tizzy. Finally I was living my dream. My mind said I was a transvestite who was smoking drugs, smoking cigarettes, and very soon was going to be satisfying "her" man. The thought of this being illegal, immoral, or wrong in any facet never crossed my path as being a bad thing. On the contrary; it became such a turn-on. It was all about me and the moment of taking what I could to satisfy myself regardless of how I used the other person.

This liaison started around 10:00 A.M. on February 22, 2005. The event lasted right into the next day until February 23 at 5:30 A.M. Soon all I cared about was smoking the pipe, smoking my cigarettes, which I chain-smoked, and getting my friend off. This was the most tunneled vision I think I ever became. I wasn't interested in food or going to the bathroom. I made sure I had enough cigarettes, so I brought three packs and went through two before I left the next morning. My friend had finally worn himself out after climbing off me for the last time. I'll never forget that time. I was lying on my back the same way I was positioned the night I was raped. I had a flashback. I wasn't sure why I felt funny about that last time he dismounted from me; however, something clicked that night that never did before. That moment would haunt me until my divine intervention.

February 23, 2005
5:30 a.m...

I remember leaving early in the morning. I was smiling. I felt that I had finally hit nirvana. I was excited. I was going back to the apartment to contact my New York connection and tell her about my session with Robert. She would surely appreciate my activities, I thought. I was still high. All I could do was fantasize in my mind; there was no reality at this point. As I pulled into the driveway of where I lived, I looked into my rearview mirror and stared at the smiling face looking back. I was finally living my fantasy as my reality, I thought. I grabbed my bags and quietly entered the apartment. I went into my bedroom and immediately got on the computer for more sex. I just wanted to scream to the world, "I have arrived! This bitch is going to rule the world!" The delusions this drug conjured up in my mind in conjunction with my addiction kept me in my fantasy for an additional twenty-four hours plus.

It was a Wednesday morning when I arrived back at my apartment. Of course, I couldn't sleep or keep my hand off my penis, which by this time was already raw from the almost twenty hours of nonstop stroking. These couple of days have taken me a while to write. Just the fact of going through it the first time was looked at from a different point of view. Today there is a lot of shame surrounding these events. I had to relive this travesty with every word I put to print. It has helped, though. It has given me insight to my behavior and the depth of my addiction. I call these final days the darkest of addiction. For the next thirty-five hours, I would continue to flash back to the events of the previous twenty-four hours. The drug is so strong, and I did so much of it that I was having residual effects that kept me in a constant state of fantasy. I didn't come out of my room to eat or go to the bathroom unless my roommate was out of the house. I looked like a druggie with my clothes all disheveled and my eyes glazed over for days. In addition, I found myself isolating so badly that my roommate knocked on the door to see if I was okay.

My actions were not to be believed. I pretended to smoke my long feminine cigarettes, taking drag after drag of unlit cigarettes until I would climax from masturbating. I tried falling asleep. I couldn't. So I would masturbate again due to flashbacks. It was a vicious cycle I couldn't stop. I wanted to stop so badly, except my mind wasn't interested. The chatter in my head kept the fantasy rolling over and over until late into the night of the twenty-third, when I was finally able to fall asleep after I masturbated for the umpteenth time. I looked pathetic. It reminded me of the vision you get watching a cop drama show where the actor is a heroin addict and just did an injection. They just sit there. That's how I looked for all the hours after I got back to my bedroom. I just lay in my bed face up, staring straight out in front of me, my mind racing minute by minute.

As I awoke on the Thursday, I was groggy, to say the least. It was about noon. My penis was shriveled and red. It hurt just looking at it. It was painful to touch. It had abrasions on both sides for most of the length that were starting to scab over. I thought about putting an antiseptic medication on; however, I remembered that it had alcohol in it. I didn't need to add fuel to the fire; I was already in enough pain. I looked in the mirror and the reflection shouted back, "You look like hell!" I had a two-day growth of beard. My breath smelled from the nearly two packs of cigarettes I had smoked a day and a half ago and brushing my teeth was not a thought then. I didn't even want a cigarette. I felt horrible. I was dehydrated. I finally showed my face to my roommate, who had been worried about me, and she asked how I felt. I lied and said that I had the flu or something. I remember it so vividly because I had never lied to her before, and I felt the pain and guilt of dishonesty run through my veins. I had to work that day. I needed to do a job for a new client. I got myself into the shower and slowly managed to clean my ravaged body. Unfortunately, it didn't help my head, which is where all the sin lay.

I was very tired. I ate a small meal and went off to do the job measure. I came back after five-something and was still tired from the morning. I said my hellos to my roommate and proceeded to eat again. I had a lot on my mind from the two days before. Reality has a cruel way of slapping you in the face when you forget it's there to begin with. That reality was that I had been in such a drug-crazed stupor that I allowed myself to engage in sexual relations without protection. Boy, did that slap hurt.

I just didn't want to think any longer, so I proceeded back to my bedroom and took myself away from pain once again by getting high on pot. It was six-thirty. I fell fast asleep. The next moment I remember was that I was awoken from a dream with the realization that God was tired of me wasting my life and wanted me to straighten up so I could do work for him. It was nine-fifteen at night on Thursday, February 24; that dream I had awoken from was a divine intervention. These five words that rolled from my lips would forever change my life: "I am a sex addict." The healing from over thirty years of emotional, physical, and psychological trauma would finally begin.

The Recovery

Recovery was my saving grace. Without recovery I could not have written these words. It might sound odd. But the truth is I wouldn't have even lived if it hadn't been for recovery.

I tell my story in my SAA group every time a newcomer comes in seeking relief and refuge from the hell of addiction. We do what is known as a mini first step in order for the newcomers to feel at ease and to let them know they really aren't alone, that we really do care for one another without judgment and work in unison to assist the group consciousness. I'll never forget that first night I walked into my first meeting. I was so ready for it. I had hit bottom and hit it hard. The only reason I was even alive was because God had better plans for me and I knew it; I just didn't know what those plans were. People who know me say I looked like the walking dead. My eyes were completely lifeless and dark. No sparkle whatsoever. I liken my appearance to that of a skid-row bum. I looked dirty. I looked a little morose. I wouldn't make eye contact with anyone. My clothes were sloppy, and I was skinny for my height. My weight was around one hundred seventy pounds. I looked like a concentration camp refugee. I was totally bankrupt in all phases of my life: emotionally, psychologically, and spiritually. The one aspect that was flourishing was my business. God saw fit to allow me to have that area grow for a little while longer.

The meeting I attended was held in the rear of a church in a classroom. It was night. God blessed these houses of worship to assist all who are ailing. Fortunately for me, I already had spiritual connection that I understood, so reconnecting was not a big hurdle. I was a bundle of emotion. Once I was able to talk, the flood gates opened with tears streaming down my face. I wasn't embarrassed. On the contrary, it was such a relief to allow myself the opportunity to shed the weight that burdened my shoulders for some thirty-odd years. I sat attentive at the end of the table as I listened very quietly as each other person took their turn and shared my experiences. I finally felt as though I found a place I belonged. They all made me feel comfortable, and no one laughed or talked back as I shared. I could see the compassion in the room. The one moment that stood out for me was the reading they shared in the beginning of the meeting. The first reading was about the purpose of the meeting. The second reading outlined what the group offered as a simple plan for recovery. This is entitled "How It Works." I followed every syllable and when it reached the part about having what others in the group already have and are willing to go to any length to get it, rockets and bells went off in my head like a Fourth of July celebration. I was being offered a way out from my own personal prison. The winning lottery numbers, except the prize you win is you get to stay alive. A "simple" program. No one said it would be easy. No one led me to believe it would be fun. However, they did say it works if you work it, so work it; you're worth it.

I didn't get the full grasp of what they were saying that night at the end prayer. I know now it works and I'm definitely worth it. In the beginning, I didn't think I was worth much of anything, to tell the truth. I had lied, cheated, stole, and basically demoralized myself nearly to death; why would anyone think I was worthy? The hard, cold fact was that this group felt I was worth it and wanted to show me why. They just said, "Keep coming back." So I took what they said to heart and came back the next week.

I started journaling my thoughts from the very first night of my epiphany. I thought it would help me reflect on my past and keep records of my feelings as I entered the gates of sobriety. It is also where I begin my reconnection with my higher power, who I fondly call Papa. You will also notice the acronym "TyF" being used; this stands for my acknowledgment of my higher power. It translates to the quote "Thank you, Father." These are my words from day one:

February 24, 2005

I'm a sex addict. I finally see it. It's 9:15 P.M. I called Caren and am waiting to hear back from her. I can't believe it's taken this long to see the truth. I'm grateful to see it. I feel FREE. I'm sad. I'm angry. I feel very angry at myself. I can't believe I hurt Lainie as I have. The lies, the deceptions. The emotional loss. I've taken all the pot and gotten rid of it. I put all of my dress-up stuff away. I put all my cigarettes in the bag and put that away as well. No more DRUGS—ever. Goodbye, lies. Goodbye, porn—hello to LIFE. I want a clean life. I want to be healthy. Tomorrow I'll see John J. at 8:00 A.M. and go to an SAA meeting. I'm tired.

This was my first night. I was so happy and sad all at the same time. I couldn't stop beating myself up for all the damage I realized I had done to my wife. What I really didn't know was that I was so close to death, it scares me even today to see this truth.

February 25, 2005

I just came from John J. He said for the first time I was being authentic with the depth of my pain. And he thought it would be good not to ever miss group again. I don't want to miss anything that is going to help me. I miss my dad. I hate seeing myself at this level. I'm in my room by myself, nothing is familiar. I feel like a skid-row bum. John gave me paperwork to attend an eight o'clock SAA meeting in Hollywood. I can't wait to pick up my first and only white chip. Doing it RIGHT or not at all. This is not a dress rehearsal. I intend to make this right from the start.
Talk later after my meeting.

Wow! I'm very grateful to God for the love He has for me. My first meeting was interesting. It was held at a church in Hollywood. There were eight of us. I was the second-youngest. I see how devastating this addiction is. One guy lost his career and wife and was raided by the FBI. I feel lucky and grateful I'm where I am. I have a chance. I'm not going to let this keep me down. I'm going to be bigger. I know it's not going to be easy; the other guys let me know that right up front. I know I'm going to feel a lot of PAIN. I don't care, I only want to get sobriety. I want a true, honest, integrity-filled life. I'm not willing to become a statistic.

I so remember that first meeting. I was a ball of emotions. I was scared and at the same time, I was calm. I was being carried by something greater than myself. It was a warmth I was familiar with in the past. I know it was my Heavenly Father cradling me in his hands. The closest illustration of how I was feeling is best described in Mary Stevenson's famous poem "Footprints in the Sand." I was also very angry, angry that a negative force controlled a large portion of my life and I wanted my life back. I was ready. It was time. This addiction had controlled my life for over twenty-five years. It owned me. However, what I saw and heard was a hope that my situation could change. I didn't have to just survive in life; I had an opportunity to start living it. I wasn't angry where I was with regards to the depth of my addiction. On the contrary, I was so grateful for the level in which I was. I was never in jail or contracted an STD. What I saw was that all of that could change very easily if I continued on my path of destruction.

February 27, 2005

I just came back from meeting Lainie. We met for coffee but ended up at a Thai restaurant. It was so painful to see her cry and let me know how much pain she was in. I know after a period of sobriety she may not want me back. The price of addiction. I'm so incensed with what I have done to her. I hope God's plans for me still hold a place for me with her. I want to be able to hold her in loving arms, giving her strength. I know I will be focusing on me for the next three to four months. I will conquer this. I'm not sure we'll be together. Only time will tell. I pray for forgiveness. I love her so much. I know she still cares for me, too. I won't stop working on me until the day I die. It's been too long since I've had any sort of stability of my own. I want to be healthy, I want to live, I want my life. It hurt so much to let Lainie go home. I have to. I can't stop crying from the emotional pain. I know God will show me the way. I've asked for love and know He will wrap me in His arms in order to give me strength no matter how painful this gets. I love you, Father. I love you. I'm going to continue reading my SLAA book. Lainie also asked me to read a book she gave me. I know it's going to be hard to read. It's called When Your Lover Is a Liar. *Goodnight.*

February 27, 2005
10:30 P.M.

I just finished reading parts from the book Lainie gave me. I'm so angry at myself for how I treated her. I will never treat another person like that ever again. I was an asshole. Never will I treat anyone like that. I believe with time I can regain the trust I so badly broke. I cried while I wrote her an email. I will have scars from this on my heart to <u>never</u> let me forget what I've done. Honestly, I'm not sure I would be happy with anyone else but her. Regardless of the past, if the future is to be one with Lainie as my wife, then I will make sure this time around she <u>never</u> has to worry about me lying. I will prevail. I may be an underdog in this battle. I intend to win anyway and have a successful, happy life as me.

Wow, what a day this was. I remember it so well. I couldn't help crying while I was with Lainie. I was a bundle of emotions. I was "raw" from emotional wounds I had seen for the first time. Just seeing her sitting there across from me, knowing how much pain she had gone through, was tearing me up inside. I was helpless. I felt like a sailboat caught in irons, neither moving forward in my life nor having the emotional strength to assist Lainie. I started to read the literature I got from the bookstore and from the meetings. I was so determined to have a life filled with happiness that I was willing to go to any length to get it. I remember the fury I had to catapult me into a healthy life. I was done living in pain, shame, and guilt. All I had to do was remember the look on Lainie's face as she got back into her car to leave me. I was crushed. You could read the pain in her face like a roadmap with big road signs saying "Beware of Sick Husband." I made a promise to myself then and there that no matter what I was going to, for the first time in my life, prevail and win. No more lies. No more deceptions.

February 28, 2005
6:45 A.M.

I woke up from a dream, but it wasn't a dream; it was real. I have been in prison that I created on myself. On February 24, 2005, I was released. The only thing is I'm alone again and on probation for the rest of my life. This is going to be the toughest, most rigorous undertaking I will ever take on...LIVING. Honestly, with integrity without exceptions. I want this. I deserve this. I have to go to work; it's 6:45 A.M.

February 28, 2005
4:00 P.M.

It's 4:00 P.M., and I feel like my head is going to explode. I have all these thoughts running through my mind about work, BNI, and SAA I have to go to a client at 5:00 P.M., and all I want to do is go home, where I belong. I want to go home. I know I cannot at this point. I know I'm accountable for all I did. My heart is heavy with shame and guilt.

Every time I think about Lainie, I have to remember I can't go backwards. I cry from the pain of remembering the lies and deceit. I know I'm not a bad person; I now know my addiction ran my life for years. The horror I caused seems like a made-for-television movie. I hope and pray that one day soon I will be strong enough to hold her again. I listened as she told me about needing a straight guy in her life. I know I'm straight. I know the drugs made me lose my inhibitions to do the acts of sex I did with men. I did the drugs to mask all the pain from earlier on. My rape pushed me over the edge. I blamed myself for so long. Then I did the drugs to mask from the lack of love from my parents growing up. Today, I know I did the drugs to mask the shame and guilt from all the hurt I caused Lainie.

After going through this FIRE, I am fine just to have a sense of me, a heterosexual man who had experimented with drugs and had anal sex with men only because I didn't know any better about my own self. I am going to get healthy so I can give myself a good life. Maybe there will be a glimmer of hope that I might be able to have a friendship or maybe even more with the one I truly love.

After my appointment at 5:00 P.M., I will be going to the Pompano Beach group's SAA meeting. Powerless of my disease moving forward one moment at a time. I love you, Papa. Before I go, I just wanted to say I will not live my life in lies or hurt anyone with lies as long as I live. I feel the pain of seeing the truth of who I was being. The end is here. LIFE will be better. I know it will; I'm committed to it. By the way, I have three days of sobriety. I can do this. I will do this.

February 28, 2005
11:15 P.M.

It's 11:15 P.M. I went to my first Pompano Beach SAA meeting and met some really nice guys. One guy was celebrating one year of sobriety. For me today was a very tough day. I had some very hard times staying in the here and now. So I was feeling a lot of pain when I would think of Lainie. Out of the group of people, I found a sponsor; his name is David. He requested I call him daily. I will and also go to meetings. I received a call from R.J. He's mad at me because I haven't called him back yet since I freaked out on him. I'll call David tomorrow and get his re-action before I call R.J. back. Doing drugs and having sex with a guy is not a good thing for me. I need my self-esteem to rise, not go down again.

I remember the day I had this dream. It was the time that I felt all the "shackles that bound me" fall to the floor. It became clear to me that I had been in the addiction for a lot of years, never really understanding the depth. I found myself emotion-ally a wreck. I was staying in touch with a few people to whom I felt I was close. As I would relate my situation, I would break down and cry over and over again. I never thought a person could cry so much. I kept thinking about going home, where I "belonged"; however, I knew this was not the answer. I had to continue to move forward in my recovery and become self-reliant. My relationship with Lainie was co-dependent and as we both knew, it would not survive even with the best of intentions.

For the first time, I was alone to live with the pain I had caused and to grieve for the losses I had experienced as I grew up. I needed to heal. It wasn't going to happen in a day or a week—that I was sure. The time I was alone was God's time to assist me in my healing. I wasn't really alone anyway. I knew I had God's grace with me all the time. I was a very fortunate person to have such a relationship with my eternal Father. I relate this time to that of the famous poem "Footprints in the Sand." I was being carried by God. I was cradled in his hands of warmth and love to protect and guide me.

It was also at this time that I met Dave, my sponsor. "My earthly guide." I waited until the meeting was over, and I walked up to Dave and managed to ask if he would be my sponsor. I was elated when he said yes. We talked for a while after the meeting, and he set up the parameters I was to follow. A phone call every day to let him know I was okay. He suggested a few books to me by Dr. Patrick Carnes, *Out of the Shadows* and *A Gentle Path through the Twelve Steps*. And gave me pamphlets about my disease to take with me and read. I went back to the apartment with a glow that night. I felt safe. I also had hope, hope that I could recover and live a "sane" life.

March 1, 2005

I was awakened to sound of two phone calls, both by R.J. I told him I was in SAA and I didn't want to talk to him for at least ninety days. I'm not gay; I'm a sex addict. He's just a guy who likes me. I called Dave and Caren and got guidance on how to handle R.J. I called Mark from my men's group, too. I see how my support network is helping me get through one day at a time. I only have a minute to write, so I wanted to jot down some thoughts. One thing I started to do is read the pamphlet on the three circles in order to understand how this cunning disease works. Later on today, I'm going to start writing down my three circles for Dave and Caren to review. I love you, Father. I'll be back later on.

Your ever-growing son.

This was a nerve-wracking day. Here I had sex with a person just over a week ago.

I then realized that the time we spent together was all related to my addiction and he wanted to continue the relationship. I didn't. I just wanted the whole relationship to disappear. I finally got the courage to call R.J. back and when I did, I explained to him that I was going to SAA and that I was a sex addict and didn't want to speak to him for at least ninety days. This was the timeframe that Caren and Dave had suggested as a time so I could get some clarity about myself and what I really wanted in my life. The truth was I wasn't sure I wanted to be friends with him any longer. More importantly, I knew if I remained friends with him, I was in immediate danger of a disease, drug overdose, or jail. I felt a sense of relief after that phone call. Later on that day, I came back to my apartment and started to read the literature I received from the meeting the previous night.

I opened the pamphlet entitled "The Three Circles." This information helped me define my sexual sobriety. It works on the premise that if I can learn to abstain from destructive and compulsive sexual behaviors, then I have a chance to learn how to maintain healthy sexual activities that are loving and nurturing. It didn't berate me into thinking I was bad or sinful; rather it outlined a very simple diagram so I could identify which of my activities were destructive and compulsive. This was done by drawing three circles on a sheet of paper, each one inside of the next, similar to a target you would use for shooting arrows. The goal is to place all those activities that are extremely destructive, e.g., picking up prostitutes or using call girl services, molestation, voyeurism, anonymous sex, exhibitionism, incest, and compulsive masturbation into the center circle. These are activities from which we abstain "one day at a time."

Then there is the outer circle. This circle represents all activities that are healthy for us and bring us back to life as opposed to the isolation in which we had been living. Such activities might include playing with our pets or children, reading recovery information, working the twelve steps, dating, enjoying a romantic dinner with a loved one, or returning back to forgotten hobbies or interests. These activities help us engage ourselves back into society. They are full of positive moments and things an addict can feel good about him or herself once more.

In between the inner and outer circle lies the middle circle. This is the area where we place those activities or behaviors about which we are uncertain. These activities or behaviors may lead us to our inner circle behaviors if compulsively acted upon. However, if managed in a positive manner, they may become outer-circle activities.

Since every person is unique, each program of recovery is individualized to meet the needs of the addict. Moving away from our inner-circle activities or behaviors on a one-day-at-a-time basis is recognized with time markers to enforce our abstinence. Additionally, with help from our sponsors, we can adjust what lies in these circles as time in abstinence lengthens. The rewards are more miraculous than any brilliance from the most beautiful faceted diamonds. Plain and simple, to an addict each day in recovery is a gift.

I have listed my three circles. It was very easy to see where I had destructive and compulsive activities and behaviors after I did this process.

What I noticed when I went through this process was that I could thread all of my inner-circle behaviors together and it all could start with just a cigarette. Amazing, you might think; however, I know it as cunning, baffling, and powerful. A disease I am powerless over. A condition that is so heinous that no one except God could assist me. I fondly call Him Papa. There actually is something good that came out of this horrid disease, and that is that I am much closer to God than I ever was.

He has drafted out a path for me to follow; He has assisted my every move. I don't make a decision without His blessings. I know that turning my will over to Him on a daily basis allows me to just manage the moment at hand. His will guides me toward the right situation or answers. That I've learned to trust with my life. Hence I say, "Thank you, Papa."

The truth of the matter is by seeing the circles for what they are, I have been able to start to create natural boundaries that in the past were very elusive. This has become a wonderful time for me because having boundaries helps keep me safe. They don't restrict me, as I once thought. I'm very grateful to know that I can let people know they are invading my space, whether it's verbal or physical, and I have learned others have boundaries as well, which allows me to learn the real meaning of respect.

March 1, 2005
9:30 P.M.

*I went to a meeting. I was at the Gay Lesbian Community Center. I wasn't sure if the time was right. As it turns out, it wasn't an SLAA meeting. It was an AA meeting. I sat in anyway. It was the original fellowship. I sat in and listened as each member spoke. I couldn't help but think how I would have traded my disease for theirs. They only had to stop drinking. I had the "keeper," the ultimate disease. I could hear the clock ticking, and all I could think of was, **Minute by minute, day by day.***

Life has slowed down a great deal. I am starting to feel feelings I never knew I had. I've become very awake to every detail of every hour; being present only reminded me how low I had sunk. The new location. The lonely nights. Thankfully, I have been growing as well. I'm grateful for that. Today my word is INTEGRITY. I'm going to go online and get information on the word. I also saw that it's the mature thing to do when you say, "I do." You put away childish thoughts and wants and live integrisously. I do without and live as my word. I only have thirty to forty years left. I want them filled with LOVE, HONOR, and INTEGRITY, not emptiness like an addict. I want my life to be RICH, PASSIONATE, and WONDROUS. When you're in your addiction, you aren't maturing or growing. You don't feel. I became devoid of intimacy. I want to learn it, love it, and share it. I want to grow old with it. I also saw that the big project I called "PEACE PARK" was actually my deepest cry for help. I was looking for inner peace...SERENITY.

It's late. I just keep staying present to the picture of Lainie, and I keep praying to God for the strength to keep growing strong to get well. I want Lainie to have a husband who is honoring her, loving her, cherishing her with INTEGRITY and wellbeing. I want that man to be me. Hopefully, someday I will be able to stand strong enough to ask her for her hand once again, only when I'm stronger. I'm maturing day by day. I will be better. TyF.

The evening was full of interesting events. I felt a little out of place while I went to the GLCC. However, I wanted to be at the meeting; I just picked the wrong time. Entering the AA room was interesting to me. I took the chair right at the door and watched as all the eyes focused on me, my face being totally unfamiliar to them.   As it is customary to do a quick go-around of who's who in the room, I acknowledged myself as "L.J. I'm a sex addict." I knew I was in a meeting room of alcoholics; however, I felt compelled to be honest about my identity. It was okay; they opened their meeting to me just the same. For the rest of the meeting, I sat and listened to the pain and sobriety of others, which gave me hope. One thing I noticed was that the disease may be different, but the pain is very much the same.

After that I went back to the apartment and fell right into my bed. Just to the left was my nightstand, which was higher than my bed. It had a space available where I had taped a picture of Lainie and me, so as I turned my head it would be facing me. I would look at it for hours at a time as I wrote in my journal. It motivated me to no end. I knew in my heart where I belonged. I also knew I had a lot of work to do learning how to live life in an honest way filled with integrity. That was all I was willing to except. I knew if I accepted anything less, I was asking for trouble. Trouble I was all too familiar with. I was very hopeful that day. I fell asleep writing in my journal.

March 2, 2005

What a fucked-up ending to an incredible day. I'm so ex-hausted from it all; I'll have to write it down tomorrow. One thing I will say is TyF for all my support because being in re-covery only since 02/25/05, I sure did want to hit the "fuck-it" button. Thankfully with my higher power at my side, nothing is worth destroying my ONLY opportunity for salva-tion and serenity. TyF; I'll talk more tomorrow.

I remember this day so vividly. I just wanted to crawl under a rock and never come out again forever. It was around eight o'clock. I had had a fantastic day. I called Lainie to talk to her and one thing led to another, and the topic of Faith (a person) had come up. This is a woman I had met at a Thanksgiving dinner with Lainie at her ex-in-laws' house. She was a friend of her ex-husband's new wife. She came dressed in what could have been called lingerie. She had dark make-up and basically looked like a call girl. Lainie and I were still together when I met this person.

However, after I separated from Lainie in January, I sought this person out to engage in sexual relations. I knew what I was doing. This is also a person Lainie asked me NOT to ever be with if we ever separated. In addiction I only heard my own inner talk say, "Go and slut around—you're free now." This woman was also a sex addict, so we fed off of each other, caring only about our-selves, never caring about anyone or anything outside of our crotches. Looking back, it was one of the worst times of my life. I was in full-blown addiction; nothing could have stopped me from this action. It's as if there is a magnet over top of you and it pulls you in the direction it wants without the ability to stop yourself in mind or body.

Well, as you might have guessed, I not only decided to be with this person, but I also felt compelled to not lie to Lainie when she asked me about it. I was standing at the window of my bedroom when Lainie asked me if I had been with Faith. I was very new to recovery; I was raw to my own wounds. It reminds me of a person whose chest is wide open for all to see the heart, lungs, and fresh meat with all the blood. It would have been better if I had taken salt and rubbed it into my chest than to have hesitated when she asked me that question. I was so intent on doing the right thing and never lying to Lainie anymore that I told the truth. I set myself up for the hell I encountered next. Lainie was so hurt, I could hear her heart break as I uttered the word "yes."

She was so angry that she swore to start the divorce proceedings at that point. I was devastated. I just took a step from the window and started to cry; the wreckage of my past had finally caught up with me, and I knew I was responsible. It was in God's hands now. I had no control over what Lainie would do. I loved her so, and the pain I caused her caused my heart to bleed with remorse over my actions. This was not a good night. I cried myself to sleep.

March 3, 2005

Well, another day, another day to be grateful for sobriety. It's late; it's 11:30 P.M. I had a very full day. All of my support came through. I spoke to Caren at 4:00 P.M. regarding the issue with Lainie. Oh yeah, I forgot to say what happened. Last night I was talking to Lainie and she requested information regarding Faith, the woman we met at Thanksgiving. I remembered the book Lainie gave me regarding lying, and I refuse to lie to her any longer.

She boxed me into a corner. She asked me if I had slept with her. After fifteen years of being together, she has a sixth sense. I hesitated for a split second and she knew I had. I then admitted to it. I could hear her heart break in two. That, she said, was the last straw between us. I'm not sure, but I feel divorce is coming next. I mean it. I went into a rage of anger with my addiction. This beast inside my head owned my life for so long. It ate at the very fabric of my being. I was its slave. I fed it daily with dishes of lies, shame, and guilt. It led me from one adult bookstore to adult bookstore. When it was really hearty, it took cocaine to quench its thirst. Empowering it into the endorphin monster it was, chasing the high longer and longer to satisfy its ever-thirsty desire for more pain.

I drove it from therapist to therapist and sat silently as it hid under the shame and guilt. "I am fine," I kept telling everyone. The dual life of lies soon would crash and burn. I was only weeks away from death. I had nothing to live for. My life was a sham. I was a sham. Not anymore, I went to an SAA tonight. My sponsor, David, asked me to stay and chat. I have been working diligently on the work at hand, putting together the three circles. I feel tired. I need to read. Just know, Father, I'm so glad you are there, loving me and giving me strength. TyF.

By the way, I shared tonight how I feel at home being able to talk openly and honestly about my addiction and how people know and understand me. They do not judge me. They too have had times like mine, not exactly—some yes, some no— but understand my pain. There is a sense of warmth and caring I felt from them toward me. I feel a few will even become friends.

There's no need to qualify what I said earlier about this situation regarding Faith; as you can see, it played havoc on my life. What I was starting to understand was that I was responsible and accountable for my own wreckage. I had to hold my breath and let the pieces fall where they will. I had bigger fish to fry. I had recovery to think about. There was nothing I was willing to put in front of my recovery, nothing. I knew I had no more chances. This was not a dress rehearsal. I felt a deep connection to my higher power, whom I fondly call Papa.

I felt warmth surrounding me in this time of despair. I was very grateful for my newfound life.

March 4, 2005
12:35 P.M.

It's 12:35 P.M., I just got off the phone with Lainie. She is filing for divorce. I'll NEVER forget this day.

March 4, 2005
6:00 P.M.

It's now 6:00 P.M. I just got back to my "cage," not prison, but a cage, nonetheless. It has no bars, it has no lock, it doesn't need them. This cage is where I go to reflect on my inner thoughts. Reflect on my shame, reflect on my loss, reflect on my life. I'm away from my home. Away from those who love me. I have to be here, it's the only place I can be alone in order to grow. Grow from my experience of my pain. The pain I feel from my years of addiction. This new awareness comes from sobriety. Thank you, Father, for the strength you give me to feel this pain and still stay the course. Your love has been my only saving grace. I know you are my only source of true unconditional love and will keep reminding myself of your will.

I keep reading the serenity prayer you have given us, and I called Lainie back at 1:30 P.M., begging for mercy from this hell I have been living in. I called not to do anything but let her know where I am and after eight days of sobriety how I feel. I told her how I was doing, how my meetings were, seeing my therapists, my men's group, and that I even went to get a new therapist who specializes in sex addiction. I will not give up on seeing how I can get well one day at a time. I will triumph. I will not live ANY LONGER IN PAIN, denial of the truth, lies, shame, or guilt.

I am immature in the area of intimacy and am willing to go to any length in order to keep my sobriety and ultimately in order to have a loving, committed, honorable, integrity-filled, monogamous relationship.

I did Breathwork today with Kari. It was very unusual. I can't explain how it works except to say as a facilitator, Kari channels God's spirit through her and assists in having my baggage exchanged with His breath. Today it opened up my senses to NEVER ALLOWING ANYONE TO EVER HARM ME AGAIN without my permission. No one can get inside my head and steal my soul. I remember the serenity prayer's first part, "Grant me the serenity to accept the things I cannot change." This refers to all my years of deception, lies, and pain

I have caused everyone and especially Lainie. In the second part, "Courage to change the things I can." This is the part that has the power for me to know I can have a healthy life. A joy-filled life. I'm not saying it is easy or will be done in a week. This may take years. I won't stop until I can be a healthy person. The phrase "never again" keeps popping up in my head. Never again give my addiction an opportunity to live, strangle it at the snake's head. Humbled to my one day at a time, one hour at a time, one minute at a time way of living. In the third part of the prayer, I will learn to "Gain the wisdom to know the difference" between the first and second part.

I love my wife, I pray a lot that as I grow in health that she will grow in health as well and we'll be together in time. Whether it's a year or two, I won't stop healing myself, not to be with Lainie, rather for me. Papa, if you feel we will be together, it will be by your will. I love you. I'm going to a meeting in Hollywood.

March 4, 2005
10:00 P.M.

It's 10:00 P.M., I just got back from my meeting. It was a good meeting. Being with others who know and understand my addiction allows me to see where I am in relationship to them. How grateful I am that I haven't been arrested for exposure or molestation like some. I can't say how sorry I am for the pain I've caused my wife. I can only feel the pain I've caused her. I'm so sorry; I've cried and continue to do so. I just want to kill the image in the mirror for hurting her. Thankfully the SAA meeting rooms have been showing me that I can feel better about myself and in time I will learn to love myself, too. I pray for that moment. I pray that I see it and can share it with someone else who is in pain from this addiction so I can serve as an inspiration like the guys in my room do for me.

I see what they have to offer me as a lottery, not a financial lottery, a bigger one that has more value. They give me the opportunity to win this lottery for FREE. I can have a healthy life. Thank you, Father. I will not stop until I win. Then I will continue and help others. I love you, Papa. Thank you for loving me. Honey, I miss you so much.

I know from the experiences from the other people that I will not make promises to my wife. I will just DO and be. From that she will see, if she is to be in my life at all. I know I have to let her go and I have. I will get well. I will grow. I will become strong. I will be happy. I will be happy. I will live. TyF

It's 12:30 A.M. I just finished with an online SLAA meeting and I got another sponsor to help me with the steps. I am going to do this work as rigorously as I can. Now I have a chance to grow four different ways. I'm crying inside with tears of joy. I have SAA meetings here in town. I have SLAA meetings online. I have my therapist and men's group. Then I have personal readings. I am going to ANY LENGTH I must in order to get recovery. What a turnaround from going to any length to create lies, deceit, and acting out. I love you, Papa, TyF, goodnight.

It was hard hearing Lainie was filing for divorce. It was part of the process. I had to swallow really hard and look at the wreckage I had left behind. I was accountable for it all. I was so angry at my addiction that by 1:30 P.M., I called Lainie back and swore my conviction that no matter where she was on the planet that I was going to find her and earn her love back. I loved her and nothing was going to come between us again unless it was by her words. Those I would respect.

The one thing I started to understand was boundaries and who had them and what they meant. So if I was not to see Lainie ever again because she requested that, then that would be the final word, the true wreckage of my addiction.

I did another Breathwork session with Kari. This type of therapy I found to be so effective. I recommend it to anyone who is truly ready to heal inside and walk their true path in life. It has almost magical powers. As I lie on my back with my eyes closed and my breathing is regulated to a faster pattern, I fall into a trancelike state. My mind opens up and emotions flow like water.

The pain that has been bottled up for decades is finally able to release out my mouth in what appears to be primal screams, thus freeing up the body of this negative energy. The result is some of the most spiritual work I've ever done. I feel a closeness to my higher power. My body feels lighter. I sense a glow in my appearance and a warmth in my heart. I fall asleep for hours after the session waking up a different person than I did when I fell asleep the night before.

By this day, I have immersed myself in recovery and therapy. I feel I have a chance to live. Without all this work, I would surely have perished and I know it. I move onto the next day even knowing my wife wants a divorce. I can't look back.

March 5, 2005
5:45 P.M.

It's 5:45 P.M. and I'm taking the time to thank God for His love. I went to my business course this morning, and the facilitator asked me how my week was. Under the circumstances of which the whole class of six know I'm in a twelve-step program. I responded that I had to go to my meetings. He responded that I didn't use the word "choice." That I could choose to go. I said, "I choose to have NO CHOICE and go to my meetings." I know I have "NO" choice. I must go. At least three to four times a week or I will die. This is not a game. He responded to me with a comment about hitting a cord with me regarding how sensitive I was toward his comment. I told him that he was not making it clear what he wanted from me. I repeated, "I choose to have no choice." I need to go. He made another remark and I said to him, "You're on dangerous ground— watch your step." He quickly responded back, "Is that a threat?" "We hit a chord inside, L.J. Maybe this is uncomfortable. You may want to check your feelings toward this class." I asked him what he meant. He said, "You may want to leave." I felt he had over stepped his boundaries with me. I picked up my belongings and did leave.

I will not let anyone get between me and my recovery. I will not let anyone try to hurt me. I'm not the twelve-year-old child

I was. I'm a man. This is my life. I get one! I intend to go to ANY LENGTH TO GET RECOVERY, which includes how a course leader feels about my choices. This is my life, FUCK this course. I really believe he was being a pompous ass. I went straight to a SAA meeting and was able to share about myself to a newcomer. That was the greatest opportunity yet. I hope and pray to you, Father, that what I said in my sharing helps someone else. A gift. That was that. I feel really good about my choice.

It's 6:30 P.M. and I have to go meet Lainie at Borders. This is going to be something. I'm not going to project. I'm just going to be. I love you, Papa, for loving me. TyF.

It's 12:10 A.M. Sunday morning. Max is chewing a bone while I'm writing. I came back from being with Lainie half an hour ago. I got to Borders early so I could look for the AA big book that my sponsor, Dave, wants me to get. They didn't have it. I left the store and to my surprise, guess who was walking up to the store, my wife, Lainie. TyF. You sent her to meet me as I was leaving. She looked spectacular. It's so nice she is blessed with beauty. She looked so relaxed and confident. She smiled as she saw me coming out. We chatted for a few minutes, then decided to go somewhere where we could sit and chat. It's late. I'm so tired. I need to go to bed. Goodnight, Papa. I love you. TyF.

After reading this passage, I remembered the morning like it was yesterday. This guy was such an arrogant bastard. As far as I was concerned, he could take the course he was teaching and shove it. I called his partner and told him point blank this guy was acting like a pompous ass. I wasn't going to return to the class. He talked me back into going. Mentally I stopped going, so it didn't matter. How dare this guy talk to me the way he did. I recognized he was challenging my boundaries. It had to stop. I did get one thing out of the course, though—a book by Eric Burne, M.D., *Games People Play*.

The best part of the day was going to my meeting. I was so mad when I left the course, but by the time the meeting was over, I had calmed down and really got back a lot from the group. The next treat I got was spending time with Lainie later that afternoon. Even though we just sat and chatted, it was a special time. We were getting to know each other all over again. By this time, I had stopped looking at her as an object and started to appreciate her for the woman she is. She was becoming a confident single woman. I could see her blossoming in her own right in a very healthy manner. While I was attending my meetings, she was attending a support group for partners of sex addicts. I was so proud of her. I really missed her.

March 6, 2005

Thank you, Papa, for another day of love and strength. Your ways keep me focused on sobriety at any costs. I couldn't wait to finish my day in order to continue writing. It's just about 8:00 P.M., and I've eaten and had some time to relax. Now it's time to get to business. First before I start, I wanted to thank you again for the miracle you blessed me with last night, having time with my wife. We talked for hours. I listened mostly as she expressed her feelings. I'm so grateful for your strength you have instilled in me thus far, and I know as day by day goes by that I know I can keep gaining. This strength allows me, as a man, to hear her pain. It cut like a knife to my core. The difference was instead of shutting her off or running like a child, I found new strength as a man to hear her.

This new strength inside has only come because of my sobriety and believing in you, a power greater than myself that could restore me to sanity. Also step number three, I made a decision to turn my will and my life over to you as I understood you. Your love for me I know is guaranteed.

We spoke for over two hours. I miss her so much. I know she is the only partner for me. I'm so in love with her. I know my sobriety comes first and if in a year or two it is to be that we are to be together, then the greatest miracle to me will have been accomplished over and above the miracles I have been having thus far. Moving along into the unknown every day, I know your might is with me.

I'll write more tomorrow. Thank you, Father, for another day of sobriety. I love you for loving me.

I felt really happy this day. I met my wife for coffee, and we sat for hours talking about her feelings and her pain. It was such a difference for me to listen to her or, more importantly, to hear her pain; no matter what I just sat and listened. There were no rebuttals. Looking back, I am amazed I sat so long with such intent. Recovery even in the earliest days showed me things I never imagined I would have done for someone else. I thank my higher power every day for the gift of listening he has shown me I can have.

March 8, 2005

Today has been a very good day. I had a business meeting at 7:30 A.M. I was on time; I kept my word. I smiled and seemed very present to the meeting. I have an SAA meeting to go to in six minutes. I'll be back after my meeting. Once again it's late…it's 11:00 P.M.

For the first time looking at my disease as an addict from a place of clarity, I get to see how things were. At nineteen I had moved out of my parents' house. My relationships with my dad, brother, and mother were poor at best. I smoked effeminate long cigarettes, smoked pot, and frequented XXX adult bookstores on a daily basis. My time at my father's business was spent smoking pot, sneaking cigarette breaks, and then at lunch, I would take off and go to a XXX adult bookstore in the next town.

By this time, I had all but isolated myself from any real friends. No one knew my truth. I was leading a double life. It got so bad that I only wanted to live my "other side"; it's where I felt I belong. I would promise myself that I wouldn't go back to the XXX movies any longer.

Then I decided to go photography school. I had tried regular college and thought it was useless for me to take the same courses over and over again, only to drop out of the course a week after it would start. The worst part was the worthless feeling I felt in my father's eyes. In order to mask the pain of feeling worthless, I began acting out over and over again. So when photography school showed up as an option, I jumped on it. I had found photography as a hobby as a teenager. I took to it like a fish to water. Although my mind would drift toward sex whenever I would get upset or frustrated, so I would get high and start taking pictures, then act out by either masturbating or going to XXX adult movies. Once again my addiction ruled. I finally took my portfolio to photography school. It was ranked number three in the country at the time. I got in.

I wanted a new start. That new start lasted less than one semester. I was an honorable mention in a Kodak-sponsored contest. It didn't stop me from acting out. The school was in Downtown Philadelphia right in the heart of the XXX adult movie houses. I was thrilled I could go any time I wanted, before school, during school, or even after school. Once again my shame and guilt got the best of me, and I couldn't concentrate on my schoolwork. I became frustrated in my "Black & White" studies course and felt very anxious. I left class and remember meeting a girl who was smoking and asked her for a cigarette. She obliged and then I asked her if she got high. She said, "Sure." Well, that was all I needed. For the next three years, all I did was get high and veg like a skid-row bum. I quit school and moved in with this girl after knowing her for a week. We fought a lot, and the sex was really bad. Sure, I did odd jobs and even got a job at a famous restaurant downtown. I was twenty-two.

One night while I was walking to my car, a man pulled up next to me and asked me if I wanted a date. I flirted with him and as an addict, I liked the intrigue of wanting to be a transvestite. This guy took me to his house and treated me very poorly. I thought I deserved it and, with my guilt and shame, performed his sexual requests. Afterwards I felt a lot of shame and drove home feeling very guilty. When I got back home to my girlfriend's place, we fought. This eventually led to the break-up of the relationship. She didn't even have a clue. I was better off without the relationship, but my addiction haunted me like bad dreams at night.

I was starting to feel as if I was getting some clarity on how my addiction that had ruled my life for so long. I also started to recount the parts of my addiction when I was between nineteen and twenty-two years old. It was interesting to see how I was starting to see the parts of my addiction, especially the part of male-to-male relationships. To see so clearly how poorly I was treated and how I realized how damning it was for me. In years past, I never believed it was a bad situation that I had gotten myself into. I thought I was doomed to lead a life as a transvestite, servicing men and aiding women of the night with their follies. I felt trapped.

To actually feel differently was a shock in and of itself. To articulate those feelings in words was a horse of another color. For the first time in my life, I had actually started to feel. I was truly feeling.

March 9, 2005

It's 6:45 P.M. It's cold and rainy. I've just come back from getting my first HIV/AIDS test. I'm very scared. I'm angry and I'm sad. I know that because of my actions there are consequences. I had sex outside of my marriage. My addiction— cunning, baffling, and powerful— led me into a nightmare world where drugs, smoking, and sex were the staples of my daily diet. Today I feel the pain of my reality. I called Lainie to check to see if she had a good session with her therapist and to see how her drive was. I know here in Ft. Lauderdale it was raining hard and the winds were fierce. I cared about how she was. This was my life now. Uncertain as it was, it affects her, too. This is where the pain is coming from. She noticed I wasn't upbeat and asked what was on my mind. I told her I was having a moment of clarity that made me sad. I know that I will not have perfectly happy days. I see the truth about life, uncertain at best, shifting moment by moment without the ability to control it. However, that doesn't mean I have to react to it. All I have is the moment I'm in.

I don't project the future while thinking about the results of my HIV test. The thought of being positive rattles my cage to no end. I'm not going to dwell on it. I can only wait the seven days until it comes back from the lab. It's eight forty-five at night; I know I stopped for dinner but didn't think time moved that fast. Tomorrow is my two-week mark of sobriety. Papa, I love you. You've given me a gift of life by hitting me with a sledgehammer of reality. I know it's me doing the work; however, I know it's your breath I breathe. You give me the courage to believe in myself. Now more than ever, I'm starting to see I must love myself in order to go through each day. I turned my will over to you. You are cradling me; I feel your love and warmth. I love you. I'm tired. I'm going to stop for today.

Talk about feeling scared. Reality hit me hard when I went to get my first HIV test. It said to me, "You had unprotected sex with someone who wasn't your wife." I started to cry. My mind started racing out of control. I wanted to cry out for help, but the one person I was looking to speak to was the one person I harmed the most. I had to physically walk this path alone for a while. I called Ed, a friend of mine, and shared my fears. He calmed me down. I was projecting the worst-case scenarios. I was projecting an estranged life with my wife. I was projecting a slow, painful death. I was so scared. I cried again before I went to sleep. I was so sorry for the pain I had caused everyone, especially Lainie. "Papa, I felt your warmth hugging me and your love cradling me," I said, and I finally went to bed. I believed in my heart of hearts that He was protecting me, but until I got the results back in seven business days, I would live in a state of uncertainty.

March 10, 2005

Today was a good day, a fulfilling day. At my meeting tonight, we talked about how we all came to being in the fellowship. There was a newcomer. It is customary when a newcomer arrives that no matter what type of meeting we're holding, whether it's an open-discussion meeting or a step meeting, that when a newcomer comes through the door that we share our own experience of how we all got there.

I shared how I got there. The truth, openly and honestly, brutally honest. Not from shame, rather from the heart. It's not pretty, not glorious. It is eye opening. It keeps reminding me how grateful I am that I'm not dead. It reminds me that I was on a collision course with death. To think I was scheduling a trip to New Jersey to become famous. I was going to make porn movies and use cocaine. I was going to kill "me." My addiction snickered at care, concern, and worry. It laughed at cause, effect, and consequences. It was refueling on shame and guilt. Lastly, it smiled at LIFEm knowing it was surely taking mine. The party train was going north, but it was never coming back.

As I said before, the truth wasn't pretty. It is the truth this disease owned me. However, this fellowship gave me the tools to win the lottery. The lottery not in monetary gains, rather winning equated to life. It has showed me a way to walk toward the light of God, my higher power. The best is it's free to use and get assistance from. A group that understands me. The one thing they ask of me is to be willing to go to <u>ANY LENGTH</u> for recovery. Let go of old habits and embrace God as I know Him to be. WOW, put all three of the items in place and I win a prize…my LIFE. A life free from the horrible pain inside. A life free from the lies and deceit I told and did to others. I'm so tired…Thank you, Papa, thank you for allowing me to be a part of your world. TyF, I love you.

Sharing my story was a great reminder of how heinous this disease truly is. How "matter of fact" it lives inside of me. Strangling my every dream or hope for a life of normalcy. I'm always amazed at the delusional thinking I had while I was in my addiction. What I find truly remarkable is how such a simple program can relieve the pain one feels inside. No one ever told me the work would be easy. They did promise, though, that as long as I followed the program, I could find peace and serenity, something I never had. I was only two weeks into recovery, and I was already learning about myself. The clarity opened my eyes to facts about myself that showed me I had been living life in such an immature manner. It didn't matter I was forty-three years old; I had been living life at the capacity of a thirteen-year-old, a childlike mentality in an adult body. This is very common among addicts. Most stopped growing emotionally due to horrible traumas in their lives at a young age. Not something God had intended for us to have to deal with as children. However, finding a spiritual path back to a God of our own understanding allows us to fill the void of a spiritual path long forgotten. This path is the ingredient to a solid recovery. The program is a spiritual-based ideology. Each and every person sets out on their own path. No one has to conform to any other person's path. Our recovery is as unique to us as our fingerprints. I relate the program to that of a lottery. Pick the right numbers, win a prize. Here you stay the course and win a prize as well, a possibility of a serene pain-free LIFE. Life will always hand out her own dishes of ups and downs. The difference is that with recovery, I learn how to live it on its own terms.

March 11, 2005

After riding the roller coaster of sexual addiction for so long as I have, it has become apparent to me since I've been in recovery that each day is a gift. Yesterday is history, tomorrow is a mystery. Right now is all I have, being present to whatever shows up, regardless of how good or bad. As I think back in order to continue with my addiction timeline, I see the cruel, depraved behavior I had toward others. I always had an agenda. The other people were just actors in a play I was producing. I fed them the lines, they fed my addiction, and my addiction would sit back and get high, dress up, and smoke cigarettes.

Nothing seems so clear than clarity over one's life. It may not be pretty. It, however, is what it is. As you heard, I had an agenda. As an active addict, I always had an agenda: "feeding my addiction." Nothing else mattered or anyone else. It was a hard truth I had to swallow as I started to get the clarity I so wanted. The analogy I used about the other people in my world was just "actors in a play I was producing." This shows the level I was at in manipulating people for my own cause. It's clear I would go to any length for my addiction. I am so sorry to all those I "used" in this production called "My Life."

March 12, 2005

Hmmm, how do I begin? Well, I just had healthy relations with my wife, Lainie. It was beautiful and odd all in the same breath. This would still be considered to be Saturday night. We went to Embassy Suites and had some tea and wine and talked. Mostly I just listened; however, there was some very nice dialogue about her feelings on my sexual affair with someone we both knew.

God bless her, Lainie, my wife, that is, to even want to look at me still baffles me. She keeps reminding me that wasn't "this me," rather the "addict me" who slept with the other person. She's not wrong. I am accountable. It's just that I'm confused in my head.

For the first time since I can remember, we had intimate relations. I was aroused—God, was I aroused. I cared about holding her, stroking her hair. The thing that gets me is that even though I was present to our relations, I could not orgasm. If I started to drift in my mind, I brought it right back to being with her. What was the cause? Was it the fact I had on a condom? Am I feeling guilt and shame? Am I that depraved that I have to have outside stimuli? I'll save these questions. I'll ask David, my sponsor. In a way, I'm still abstaining. My wife, she was radiant, loving and insightful with her conversation. It was exciting when she asked me to stay over. I'm confused as to how my body reacted to this evening. Caren can help me. Papa, I love you. Thank you for watching over me and giving love and everlasting guidance. I believe I'm still ashamed.

What an incredible night this was. It was a miracle as far as I was concerned. Lainie looked so beautiful. It was fantastic how well she was taking care of herself. What started out as a simple casual drink turned into a romantic interlude. I was very aroused by the thought of us being together. Part of being in recovery meant being responsible sexually, which meant that I had to wear a condom. I didn't mind one bit. As far as I was concerned, I could care less about having sex. I was much more interested in being intimate, holding her in my arms close to my heart, caressing her skin next to mine. Stroking her golden locks as I just smelled her scent. This was what I cared about.

It was different for me this time around, and I was so glad that God had blessed me with such a chance. I considered it to be a miracle. As far as my inability to reach orgasm, I really wasn't all that concerned. I was in a new place. It was totally unchartered water for me. I knew in God's time I would reach orgasm, or I wouldn't if that was God's will for me. All I cared about was being back with my wife as a husband, an intimate companion, and as a friend. This meant more than any three seconds of ecstasy. I felt so blessed this day and if God saw fit to take me, then I would have had all that I ever could have asked for. I was truly a blessed man.

March 13, 2005

I lay in bed with Lainie for six hours. It was beautiful. I did sleep a little. I tossed a lot. Even though I didn't climax, I had healthy relations with my wife. It was a beautiful, intimate evening. I was very focused in the adult state with being present in the moment as the most important thought. TyF. I am on the Broward Blvd / I95 overpass...what an amazing sunrise. Thank you, Papa. I'll write later on.

It's 7:50 P.M. I'm still thinking about last night and how wonderful it was to feel so close and intimate while still knowing I'm an addict. I am; it's okay. Embracing the truth and admitting I'm powerless created such freedom. Turning my will over to you, Papa, every day assists in my growth in knowledge, intimacy, relationship, integrity, fun, and a whole world that before I was shut off from.

Looking back, I see how I snatched away positive energy from a lot of people all to satisfy my own disease. At twenty-three, I really got into my own disease by putting on another mask and becoming a male stripper, further isolating myself. I never had sex with anyone I did a show for; however, I did "use" myself to expose myself in public. Not totally nude—close enough, though. I had become an exhibitionist. I further isolated myself. I would not date. I became a sexual anorexia. I was only with myself, over and over. Being a stripper was a perfect cover to act out daily by masturbating, smoking, and getting high. I continued to beat myself up with shame and guilt. I continued to see the guy who liked me to dress up. As I look back, he was so abusive to me verbally by calling me "whore" and "cock-sucking bitch," and I kept going back for more. I thought it was where I belonged, and I was getting what I deserved. After all, I was a transvestite, so I thought I loved dressing up. I was supposed to service men. I was doing what I needed to do in order to get the love and attention from men.

I had an efficiency apartment. My friends had no clue who I was. We'd all get high together, then I would sneak off back to my apartment to masturbate while smoking and watching myself smoke in the mirror with lipstick on. The thought I am a woman *never left me. I would swear to myself that I would stop smoking, stop dressing, stop seeing that one guy who had me have sex with other guys while he watched. I was so high, I didn't care. I was supposed to be there, I thought. This is what I deserved in life. I couldn't understand why I hated myself every time I had an orgasm. I would immediately go right back to my male personality, all my female clothes came off. The lipstick—gone. The heels—off. As I write this, I can't believe this disease ran my life like it did. I couldn't understand why I felt like I was twelve years old all the time. Like I never grew up. Today after much therapy and Breathwork, I know I'm a young man who is an addict, not a confused twelve-year-old.*

I can still see in my mind's eye that Sunday morning as I was driving back to the apartment. I had a big smile on my face. I was in wonderment of such a beautiful sunrise as it peeked up through the skyscrapers in Downtown Ft. Lauderdale. God in his ultimate wisdom saw fit to make sunrises so beautiful for all to see. I felt blessed that morning. It was the perfect ending to a wonderful evening. My wife was so amazing. Her look, her talk, her warmth, her scent. She drove me crazy. I knew I was with the right person for me. She is the only woman for me.

I continued to look back at my sexual history and started to feel dirty from all the exhibitionism I had done over my five-year career as a stripper. I never looked at myself as an exhibitionist. I was getting such clarity that day, I could see it as plain as day. For so long, I thought I was doing a service to women when, in fact, I was doing a dis-service to myself. Funny how an addiction could warp my mind into becoming delusional. I was in such denial.

Then I started to look at being with Michael again. How I allowed myself to become so subservient and verbally abused, never mind the sexual abuse. For the first time, I was questioning my actions and behaviors with Michael. It made me feel extremely sick in my stomach and really angry to know that I was victimized as I was. I was truly taken advantage of. He was a predator. I finally knew what that meant.

March 14, 2005

Today was a beautiful day. Papa, if you had taken me today, you would have given me another beautiful day. For that I am grateful. I know my days are truly limited, and I see by your guidance I am here to assist others, period. As I continue to look back at my addiction timeline, I recognize I've hurt others for my own selfish gains. My addiction was ferocious with its appetite. As a stripper, I did over three thousand solo performances in five years. However, I drew the line in the sand when I was asked to do a party for a Latin girl who was turning fifteen. As far as I was concerned, she was too young for such "adult" fun. I'm falling again. Goodnight, Papa. I love you.

What can you say when you look at each day as a gift? I realized as each day passed how precious each day was. Not by just saying it, rather by feeling it. I had come to grips with my mortality, and the fact that each day I was alive was a present. A miracle for my mind, body, and soul to revel in, soaking up as much as I could, living with integrity, honor, and love. I really, truly was starting to walk this spiritual path, I knew it, and more importantly, I was deeply grateful for it.

Again I was re-accounting my sexual timeline. It's so hard to imagine I performed as much as I did. I don't regret this part of my life; however, I do recognize it was not healthy behavior.

Funny as it is, I, a sex addict in total addiction, consciously recognized abuse of another, but I could not see my own abuse even when it slapped me in the face. Not anymore.

March 15, 2005

It's 5:45 A.M. and the beginning of another day. First I want to thank you, Papa…I'm not waking up in the middle of the night, sweating, wondering who I told my last lie to or rushing out early to get to my first video. What a lonely way of being. Instead I'm getting to do a moment of "clean" meditation followed by a business meeting. I love you. Thank you for the clarity you are allowing me to have and the gift of life in all its wondrous ways.

I am an addict. I am blessed to have another day alive. TyF. I'll chat later.

It's 6:45 P.M. I just got back to my apartment after going to the HIV testing facility one day earlier in hopes of getting my first results back. I once again was brought to my knees in understanding of how deep my addiction sank my life. A reality so vivid I cried, the realization of possibly having to explain to my wife that I'm HIV positive. Papa, I am on my knees in my heart and mind, begging for your mercy and allowing me to be HIV-free. Not that if I am positive that I will turn around and act out once again. On the contrary, this will allow me to have normal relations with my wife. I am one hundred percent in your will as we speak. It is my intention to place you above all on a daily basis, and as I understand more of your wisdom.

Going back to my timeline brings me to a very important part. I was twenty-five, two years into stripping with no "real" relationships until I met a girl who was extremely immature and sheltered. She was eight years older than me. I told her I wanted to marry her. I was nuts to even think I was mature enough to understand the concept of marriage. I broke off the relationship when I realized I was too immature. I knew it. I thought looking back that it was her fault. She didn't under-

stand me. What I did was for the best. At least I only broke her heart once, not like my wife, who I destroyed her faith in me, her self image as a wife, and the trust.

So I packed my bags and moved to Ft. Lauderdale, Florida, in April 1986. I got a room with this older guy who was a financial wiz kid in his seventies after being introduced to him on my first trip down to Florida a month earlier. He had an extra room, and I just had to get out of Philadelphia. I didn't know the gentleman was gay. I found out later on as well as that he was very controlling. He would get very upset with me because I didn't want to hang out with him and his friends going to bars to meet other gay men. "Sorry," I said. It wasn't my lifestyle. So within six months, I had met another woman and moved in with her. It's late, I'm falling asleep. Goodnight, Papa. I love you. TyF.

It was clear to see how appreciative I was to my higher power for allowing me to have another day. This meant a lot to me, more than you know. So I did what I could to get the information regarding my HIV test. Unfortunately the lab didn't have results yet. I kept praying day and night for a healthy life.

As I continued on my timeline, I almost forgot about the relationship I had, which was a catalyst for me to move. To this day, I don't remember her name. What I do remember is the guilt of my lifestyle at that time was so painful that I thought I had to leave in order to spare her the pain of the truth. After all, I figured a new location could help me start a new life. The truth is though, when I packed my bags to move to Ft. Lauderdale, my addiction packed its own bags and moved with me. It never told me it was coming. I thought I was finally free, and I was for a short period of time. My new roommate kept me very busy. Then things started to change and once again, I was smoking, getting high, and going to XXX adult bookstores. Recovery showed me I was still in my addiction. Back then I never knew. I just thought I had found a better place to have fun.

Another point that had become clear to me was the pattern of relationships I had had, constantly jumping from one to another without any concern for the other person. It was all about me.

March 16, 2005

This is going down as one of the happiest days since I acknowledged I was an addict. I got my HIV test back. TyF. It was negative. I'm so grateful, Papa. I love you. I will be going online to a meeting, then I'm going to bed. I will be off tomorrow in the morning, so I intend to write and read. I am at your feet, on my knees, grateful for your love for me.

I almost jumped to the moon with gratitude for this day. I was HIV negative. I started to cry tears of joy on the way home from the testing facility. I called Lainie right away and let her know. This was the first hurdle of three tests I had to take. The good part was this first part is generally a good indicator of the rest of the results. Papa, I was grateful then and I'm extremely grateful today, a year and five months later. Papa, your love and warmth has been the guidance I've used to keep me on the path that is your will for me. Thank you for your love. Your humble son, me.

March 17, 2005

Papa, I've got to tell you I was intent on sleeping in, well...I have been given such a renewed energy for life through you that I did not read at all today because I was working instead. Now it's 8:45 P.M. I am home after I went to a meeting. It was awesome. I'm going to eat. Oh, my...Papa, the miracles you have bestowed upon me. I just got a call from Lainie. She just came home from her first COSA meeting. It's 9:30 P.M. I was worried with the weather being really rainy and her driving. I called her cell and left a message for her to call me to let me know she was okay. Papa, I love you so much for bringing to a path that leads to sanity, allowing me to find the courage to admit the truth to myself that I am a sex addict. Allowing me to stop acting out. Ultimately leading me to the possibility of life, not DEATH, like I was headed toward.

Your love has cradled me to see my pain, my wrongs, myself. I love you. I love you. TyF.

I always thought if there was going to be an "us," it was because Lainie took the time to do work for herself. Growth was an integral part of our recovery for both of us. It took a lot of courage for me to walk the path I was on. As far as I was concerned, it took even more courage for the partner of a sex addict to look for help. Putting back their life is so helpful to their well-being. Just for a minute, think of how negatively this disease has impacted a partner's life by ripping apart their core beliefs of themselves, mostly leaving them in emotional and psychological shambles. I was so proud of Lainie for choosing her own path for her own recovery for her, not for me. Each of us must do it for ourselves; no one can do it for us or its results don't penetrate to the depth they need to be. I always feel bad for those newcomers who come into the rooms stating that they are there to satisfy their wives or partners; they're not doing recovery for themselves. They either change their conversation or stop coming. It's a sad but true fact.

March 18, 2005

Three weeks of sobriety today! I love you, Papa. Your wisdom has enabled me to learn to LIVE. Living is all I want to do. Today, more than any other, I have caught of true joy for me. I was talking to Lainie regarding my stepdaughter. Lainie was describing her conversation regarding COSA and my SAA and my addiction. What I saw was through this horrific disease when a family has a strong core bond of love that the relationship of truth and love gets deeper. What I'm trying to express is that because I'm an addict and I'm in recovery, I'm growing healthy as a person. I directly affect Lainie, my wife. She in turn is seeking assistance to cope with my addiction and has found COSA, a support group where she talks to others who are spouses or partners of sex addicts. She is in a safe place. Thank you, Papa, for creating a safe place for her. She is making it a point to grow from this horrific event.

She has taken a stand for herself to gain emotional and psychological strength in order to understand herself better and to never become a victim again. I'm so proud of her for pur-

suing this. Papa, she means the world to me. To see her grow from this chaos into a stronger person because of this disease gives me great joy. It means to me that a wonderful person just polished her edges. Honey, I love you so much, one day at a time with a healthy, loving partner. Papa, I love you for putting us together. I will forever treasure this moment in time. Your humble servant, me.

"Three weeks." Wow! I would have never thought I could do this. I was on to something. I saw changes in me. I felt different than three weeks ago. They say I was on this "pink cloud," a way of saying reality hasn't hit yet. It's where you feel so good emotionally and psychologically since coming into recovery. Each person is different; however, this "pink cloud" can last for weeks and weeks. I was loving this good feeling.

Additionally, Lainie was going to her group. Her group was put together by a therapist who created it for partners of sex addicts. I think it is a wonderful group. I call it COSA. There are real groups set up for partners, that is on a national level; it is called COSA. They can be found on the internet at *http://www.cosa-recovery.org*. I believe every person involved in the addiction as a partner should take advantage of such a group. Getting back your sanity is worth everything.

March 19, 2005

What to say…I'm so in love with today, Papa. It was fantastic. I see how by taking each waking moment and feeling its impact allows me to better appreciate the days gone by. It's late, almost 1:00 A.M. I'm with Lainie in our bed. We just made love. I even reached a climax. There is such a dramatic difference in being "present" in the moment, feeling every second of her, instead of being in my head about lies and deceit. I'm very tired now. I need to say I love you, TyF.

What a great feeling to be in love with a day, being present to all that surrounds you. Then to have the greatest gift of all, making love as the crème de la crème as the last part of your day.

Don't get me wrong; this isn't about the sex, it's about the day in of itself. The gift of being so present in each and every moment as not to miss anything that is going on in your presence. Taking a walk and looking up and seeing and hearing the call of an osprey or smelling the freshly cut grass or touching the bark of the tree on your street, being so in the moment that nothing escapes your senses. That's why I appreciated this day so much. It filled all my senses to overflowing, and it felt great not to miss any of what God wanted to share with me. This was only possible because I am in recovery. Most of what happened today I would have missed because in my addiction, I was so engrossed in outside stimuli that if a million dollars had fallen from the sky, I would have missed that, too.

March 20, 2005

A twelve-lion roar…from the depth of my faith, which I feel is like the twelve tribes of Israel, hence the twelve-lion roar. I scream to you how much I love you. Papa, I love you. I've been looking back at my timeline and want to pick up where I left off. Getting back to when I was living with this guy, Ray, I found out he was very upset I was leaving him.

My pattern for "using" people continued. This girl I moved in with was self-sufficient. I am attracted to women who are strong. As it turned out, she was naïve, which was good for me since I had my addiction to think of. I just never looked at it that way before. It had a mind of its own.

I was two and a half years into stripping when I met her. She never suspected my addiction, and being out late for work never sent up any red flags. I had created the "perfect" lifestyle, so I thought. I worked when I could and then after would drive from adult bookstore to adult bookstore without anyone being suspicious. Looking back, it's so plain to see the destructive nature of my relationships, although I was blind as a bat. This relationship based mostly on sex was doomed as the pasted ones. As my diet for transsexual videos and pornography grew, so did my shame and guilt and desires to act out.

I wanted, so I thought, to be penetrated anally so bad that one day I brought home a dildo and asked my girlfriend to penetrate me. She wasn't into it and thought I was a little weird. I left her after I met a new girl who worked next to my current girlfriend's business. It wasn't long before I started flirting with the new girl, and soon my relationship with my current girlfriend ended. True to tradition, I moved out.

I managed to keep my relationship with this new girlfriend. We spent long nights chatting. I was still stripping, and she had a candy basket business, so I thought we complemented each other. We talked until late at night, often talking about how much I hated sex and that I wished sex didn't exist. Was I on a path of understanding my addiction? No way. I was drawing in my next bad relationship. The only issue was this girl was smart. This courtship was short and sweet. Her parents seemed to like me, too. I was Jewish, and so was she. She was demanding, I showed her attention and in return, I was given a roof over my head. We moved into her parents' house. The truth is I never left; I just kept coming back. Sound familiar? I love you, Papa. I'm so tired.

The "pink cloud" was a beautiful place to be. I felt so blissful. I just kept thanking my higher power for the gift of another day alive and with just that little extra gift of understanding myself a little more.

Looking deeper into my timeline, I'm almost present date. The relationship I ended in was a true test of my will. The woman had two young daughters, neither of whom I could handle. They were thirteen and nine when I first met their mother. Their mother had a revolving door set up for her boyfriends. I was just another one on the trail; however, I was one of a few who moved in to her house. The children by this time already grew accustomed to their mother's business hours and were latchkey kids at best. I fit right in. My history and addiction was perfectly matched for this dysfunctional relationship. The relationship had no chance of ever going anywhere. I was too blind to see past my own needs to seriously care about anyone else.

Then as my addiction grew stronger and I started to isolate more, I pulled further away from my responsibilities and the relationship until I had nothing except myself in a lonely video booth for hours upon hours. The sad ending to all of my relationships has ended in the same fashion as I look back. That's when I would go into a tirade about hating sex as I did after I had met my ex-wife. She was the last relationship I had before I went down into dark depths of my addiction. Once again, I managed to find a person who conveniently had all of the staples I needed in order to survive. Notice I said "survive." That's all I was doing was surviving. My ex-wife lived at her parents' house, she made a decent buck, and she was a perfect life raft for my overboard lifestyle. She condoned my stripping and even became an agent for me, booking me for shows, and because of my Jewish Philadelphia background, I was taken in by her parents as well. I had them all fooled. What a vicious black hole I felt I was drifting toward, and what was worse was I couldn't stop myself from acting out. Not one bit. I felt terribly lonely even lying in the same bed as my ex-wife. I felt cold and alone. I hated my life and started looking for a way out, again.

March 21, 2005

Can you believe it's the twenty-first already? I'm shocked at how fast time has flown by. Tonight was my meeting, and it was awesome. It's 11:20 P.M., Papa, and I'm so tired. I hear a train whistle blow out in the distant outside air. I am so grateful I can still hear at all. I will write tomorrow before I drop the pen. Honey, I love you. I close my eyes and see your blue eyes looking at me. I melt. I cry inside and out with tears of joy. I pray that I never wake up from this dream.

Almost a month into recovery, the time has flown by. I have a renewed energy for life that I use until I almost pass out at the end of each day. As you can hear, I'm so exhausted from the day's activities, I can hardly keep the pen up. It was a long day. I'm looking at the picture of Lainie I taped to my nightstand, and I drift into a fantasy of her looking at me with a smile on her face.

I cry inside and out; the tears of joy roll down my face. I put away my journal. I fall asleep.

March 22, 2005

It's ten until two in the afternoon, and I've already been to two appointments and have spoken to my sponsor, Dave, and two other people in group. What I've noticed is how my thinking has changed regarding sexual addiction. I have embraced it fully. Since I have embraced my addiction and except its many faces, I have been freed to start a new life. Papa, you know who I am. I bow down at your feet. I've turned my will over to you. I pray for your guidance every day. As you have been answering my questions, I have been noticing a renewed sense of self-assurance and inner strength to recognize and distinguish actions, thoughts, and ideas around sex that used to cloud my thoughts.

I see how my addiction drove me to use drugs, commit adultery, and create thoughts of suicide. The times I used cocaine while I was married did not take away the pain I was feeling inside; it drove me to commit acts of which I was even more shameful and guilty. It took me to the edge of death. It created the illusion in my mind that dressing as a woman, complete with pierced ears, full make-up, wearing a mini-skirt, thigh-highs, and five-inch heels, was the way of life I had been missing. I remember dressing up and literally driving to an adult theater, going inside, smoking long effeminate cigarettes, and purposely trying to attract men for sex. High on cocaine was the" be all to end all" for me. In my mind, I was a "coke whore." I wanted to be a coke whore so badly that I <u>had</u> to do it.

I craved the attention I so lacked and thought I deserved.

The drugs and the addiction were best friends; they drove each other to the edge, and I was the pawn. The twelve-year-old who was confused and unsure was now a "woman" who knew what she wanted. I knew how to treat men. I knew how to manipulate them. I was going to use my "sexy female" attitude to show them who was boss. Then I climaxed. However, instead of stopping, I craved more, more of everything. The coke enticed the addict, the addict ran the show, and the twelve-year-old got pushed around in a haze of shame and guilt.

I now know that all my behavior from as early as twelve or so until I declared my addiction on February 24, 2005, to be exact, was all tied to SEXUAL ADDICTION. I will not regret it, nor wish to shut the door on it. I know I need to live with these memories for the rest of my life; however, I have chosen not to repeat it again. I know that if I ever touch my inner circle of activities again in this lifetime, it can kill me. There is no second chance, there is no alternative. Just death, plain and simple. The most incredible thing to me is that for all my teens, twenties, thirties, and early forties, I have rarely been completely present to people around me. Not much authenticity in my relationships. I found myself drifting off to events, people, places, or things dealing with sex. This is the first time I have felt good about myself. I'm not saying I'm feeling perfect or even half perfect. I just feel okay for today, one day at a time. I love you, Papa. I'm tired.

It had taken close to a month to come to the terms regarding my addiction. I saw that embracing the addiction as opposed to rejecting it allowed me to live in peace with it. If I had rejected it, I would again be in denial and probably in active addiction. By coming to terms with it, I was now living in harmony with it, which gave no power to life. I had become clearer that my behaviors not only were demonic in nature also had a mind of their own. Remembering the times I went to the adult theater all dressed as a woman truly showed the delusional strength my addiction had over my conscious mind. Mostly the realization that I had been in addiction for the later part of my teens, all of my twenties, thirties, and the beginning of my forties made me pause to feel the depth of how insane my life had become. I paused again and gave thanks that I was still alive. I felt okay. It felt okay to be okay. I smiled and went to sleep, knowing I was safe for another day.

March 23, 2005

Papa, its 11:45 P.M. Fifteen more minutes, and I have completed my first month of sobriety. Thank you for your love, your guidance, your wisdom. I'm very clear knowing your love for me is eternal that as I lift my eyes up toward you, I'm no longer blinded by shame or guilt; rather I feel your love and warmth of conviction. I love you, TyE. I know I could not have done my work without you. I am eternally grateful to you for sparing my life and allowing me to feel the beauty life is and can be. Goodnight. I'm tired.

I was so excited, for it was my first month of sobriety. The first time I ever stuck with something that was good for me. I felt that I belonged to this group. A group of men and sometimes women who offered me support and understanding unlike anyone else ever did. Finally I was on a positive path to better my life without any secrets. I was so grateful.

March 26, 2005

Papa, thank you for allowing me to look inside myself. Thank you for giving me the courage to see myself as I am. To look at my faults that I have, to see the way I have been in the past. The lies, the deceit, and the theft of love from people who put out their arms without fear. I have been very present to feeling the pain when I look at those I've harmed.

Now as I reflect back and now as I live presently, I see how each day I grow in heart, mind, and soul. As you have requested, I'm giving back serving you. I now chair the Saturday meeting of SAA. I feel you through my body as I tell my story of how I arrived in these rooms that have saved me. I feel good today, stronger than yesterday. Last night you gave me another miracle, another day alive. Another day to share with my wife. I can't tell you how grateful I am that you spared my life. I was in so much pain for so many years. You and you alone have given me the courage to live and feel life again. To live without shame and guilt, to honor my wife, to honor my marriage, and to keep holy the sanctity of my vows. Oh, Father, I love you for never abandoning me and for giving me the courage to see how my past was destroying me. The most important is seeing the truth of my addiction. Papa, I love you. TyF.

I felt so much gratitude for the ability to see myself for who I was. It's true: I was in recovery for a short period; however, I was becoming enlightened a little more each and every day. I was still floating on this so-called "pink cloud," and I was starting to see that recovery was even transcending to my work environment as well. I was very grateful for the so-called "pink cloud."

March 27, 2005

I read a line in my Out of the Shadows *book by Patrick Carnes, which really struck a chord in me. It was on page seventy-eight, the beginning of paragraph three. It said, "In every life there are moments of extraordinary clarity." I saw that line and it reminded me of the moment I realized I was a sex addict. My life was unmanageable and I wanted help. As I look back years ago, before my stepdaughter moved in with my wife and me, I found cybersex. I knew it was wrong to be viewing it from the very beginning. That created a bigger rush.*

I remember one night it was late. I couldn't sleep, so I got up and went into my office and got onto the computer and started browsing transsexual websites. I was so entranced, I lost track of time. My wife woke up and turned the knob of my office and the door was locked. She requested entrance. I froze, I unlocked the door. She came in and saw that my crotch looked aroused and that I left the information on the screen. I was caught masturbating without the evidence, my physical presence told the story. That was the first of a few times I got caught. I swore to never do it again as my mind was devising ways to do it again as I was lying to her at that moment. It was sickening to see as I reflected back. Reading these books on sexual addiction has brought so much clarity to light that I find it difficult to imagine what my life would have looked like if I had had sobriety ten years earlier. I can wish and pray, reality said NOW was the time for me. TyF.

I'm going to put away this journal for the night and leave with a special note. My dear wife, Lainie, and I had a special day together, under some trees, on a bank of a canal, just watching boats float by as I cherished her scent, touch, and gaze that fell upon me. TyF, Papa, for it was truly a blessed day for me. I love you.

I talk about a book I received, *Out of the Shadows,* by Patrick Carnes. This was the greatest database for understanding the mechanics of my disease. It answered the how, what, and why of my disease. A disease that has no cure, is progressive and deadly, a disease so cunning, baffling, and powerful that only my higher power can assist me with my recovery.

Then there were the days I was caught up on the web masturbating while looking at transsexual porn sites, not ever thinking my wife would wander into the room. What a fool I was to think I was actually getting away with something, then to lie straight to her face while I swore I'd never do it again. The interesting thing was watching my brain, even while I was talking to my wife, trying to circumvent getting caught again and still viewing the porn. I felt criminal, low, and disgusting.

What was nice is how we found a quiet bank along a canal and laid out a blanket and sat and enjoyed each other's company. It was a day out of a romance movie. The love was flowing. I felt so blessed for that day. It was a miracle in itself. Actually, this type of situation wouldn't have taken place before because I didn't want to spend the time with my wife. So this was in far contrast to my previous years. This was recovery working in my life. It was a beautiful day.

March 28, 2005

As I look back and rewind my life of addiction, I'm looking at the last straw that broke my heart in two. I'll never forget it, nor will I ever wish to experience such pain brought on by myself, to the person I claimed to love the most, my wife. I'm not sure of the exact day it all happened, I can say it was in January 2005. I was on a website for people looking to hook up for alternative lifestyle sexual relationships. At this point in my life, I wasn't sure if I was gay, straight, or bi. I wasn't sure if I wanted to be male, female, or a transsexual. My addiction had me completely baffled. I had an extreme amount of guilt and shame. My head and heart swirled in denial. I wanted it all, and I thought in my present situation, I was married to the wrong woman.

I created a profile for this website. It said something to the effect, "Bi male, loves to dress, smoking fetish, wife doesn't appreciate me. See if you can steal me away." This is not exact, but it's close. Getting back to that fateful day…in the morning I was online. I left a window open on the computer and didn't know it. My stepdaughter went on the computer at night and saw the site I was on and showed it to my wife. My wife printed all of the communications I had from the site. She called me and very calmly asked me to meet her at Barnes & Noble, where we always go. She was very calm, and I had no idea anything was wrong. As I write this, my stomach turns at the despicable nature of my addiction. Cunning, baffling, and powerful. I finally met Lainie in the parking lot of Barnes & Noble. I'm not sure what time it was, somewhere around seven at night. She was relaxed. She was sitting in her car and motioned for me to come to her car. I did. She said, "Hello," then handed me the papers she printed off the net.

I remember the feeling of despair, horror, and disbelief come over me. My secret double life came crashing down around me right there in the seat next to my wife. I didn't know where to turn. My head went into a swirl. My twelve-year-old mind was kicking and screaming. Everywhere I reached, I hit the sides of the "bubble." The bubble is a term used to describe what an addict feels when in active addiction. Imagine being engulfed by a large bubble and being in a powerless compulsion of acting out in your addiction and not being able to communicate realistically with the outside world because the walls around you are cut off. I was helpless. I was in so much pain and shame,

*and I was guilt-ridden. My mind thought of suicide to end all
the pain.*

What a horrible day. I wanted to crawl up into a ball like an
armadillo and roll away, forever. I remember writing this moment
in my journal. I started to cry. I was so mad at my stepdaughter
and harbored a lot of resentment toward her. Of course, being in
recovery for nineteen months, I've come to see the resentment
was pointed in the wrong direction. As they say, when you point
a finger at someone, three fingers point back at you. It was totally
my fault. I wasn't man enough to take responsibility for my actions. Today it's a different story, and I have made peace with my
stepdaughter. I'm truly blessed by her relationship and thank God
for her strong moral beliefs.

The night all this transpired, I was so scared. I immediately
went into a childlike state and started lashing out at the air,
screaming, "No, no, no!" I wanted my dad to reach out and hug
me and tell me everything was going to be okay. Of course, since
his death, nothing seemed to be going right, and this night was
the epitome of the horrific pain I could cause. More horrifying
was the fact it was happening to the one person I claimed I loved
the most. There was no reason to live any longer; I had hit the
most painful part in my relationship to date. We didn't speak the
rest of the night. Three days later, I moved out.

March 29, 2005

*Papa, I'm so grateful you have given me another day. It's
11:00 at night. I just finished working out my body at the gym,
my temple of my soul, which houses no guilt from lies or deceit.
Every day I "feel" more and more. I "see" more and more. I feel
that I grow just a little more each day, not a lot, just a little.
It's okay. Papa, each day I feel a little more confident in my
sexuality. I'm forty-three and I don't make any bones about it.
I can't tell you how good it feels to not feel confused about my
sexuality. Every day that goes by allows me to grow internally
in my heart, into the man I know I am. What I naturally feel
that I am. If the truth for me was that I felt gay, then gay I'd*

be. However, I don't. I feel very much heterosexual. The fact that I understand what it feels like to be penetrated anally doesn't mean I'm homosexual. It just means that I have a knowingness. I'm glad I'm not confused about that any longer. I like being a man. I love you, Papa. I'm tired. TyF. Goodnight.

This day marked a very important moment in my newly conscious adult life. I had come to terms with my sexuality. It didn't matter that for twenty-five years I had sought out the same sex or that I physically understood the feelings of anal intercourse. What it meant was that I was free from the bondage of thinking I was doomed to live a life that neither appealed to me nor felt good. I was freed to the conscious understanding that my sexuality was not dictated by my past addictive actions. That I was indeed a heterosexual male and forgiving myself for past experiences would allow for the healing to begin. Healing I needed to soothe my scared, wounded soul.

March 30, 2005

Today I felt bad for Lainie. Her ex-sister-in-law was harping on her that she needed to get rid of me. Robin, my step-daughter, saw a message I left in my wife's eyeglass case, and she was upset with Lainie as well. I understand, Papa...I'm so tired...I would write more but I'm exhausted.

What a day this day was. I couldn't believe that everyone was ganging up on my wife. She didn't need any undue stress. We had enough to deal with in our lives. I understood where the people were coming from. They thought I was scum. I accept that, but they weren't in my shoes; they weren't in my head. Lainie is the only one who truly knew me. She knew the pain I was in. She saw the years of suffering I went through. People only saw what was on the surface. On the surface, it looked really bad. I would have hated me as well. Today, I know differently. I know I have an incurable disease of the mind. I also have two mental disorders, which doesn't help either, but I have hope. By the grace of God, I have medication for my mental disorders, and I have a twelve-step recovery program for my disease. The fact that I can be an addict in recovery and on medication is a far better thought than the inevitable, which would be death, if I didn't have both these preventives to save me. I love you, Papa, for your gifts are beyond compare.

March 31, 2005

Wow, look how I left last night. I was so tired. I can't say that I'm so far behind last night's tiredness. Today was a very nice day. I saw a rainbow cloud, my first at six-forty this morning. It's so late. I've been running since five this morning. I'm fading fast. Goodnight, Papa.

There's not really much to say about this day. I said it so clearly. I was wiped out. In those days, I was working doing installs of custom closets, going to meetings at night, then working out at a steel gym for about two hours afterwards. I'd get home and make my dinner sometimes at eleven at night. Then I would read some recovery materials and then lastly write in my journal most of the time while I was lying in my bed ready for sleep. My days were very full in my beginning months of recovery. I'm glad, too. As I started this journey, I wanted to make sure my focus was on recovery first. I did this because without recovery being first in my life, it left an opening for my addiction to come back, and that was the last thing I wanted.

April 3, 2005

It's 6:42 P.M. I'm watching the movie Ghost. *Papa, I am so grateful for your love and guidance. It's the end of the movie. I'm on my knees, humbly thanking you for your love. I will be your humble servant in whatever calling you want of me. Thank you for allowing me to share my wife's love. You are my forever guide here and beyond. Looking back at this weekend, I spent it all with Lainie, very present. What a gift.*

It's now 11:00 P.M., and I just watched a program called Intervention. *It was about a girl who was a crystal meth addict. I saw myself in that person. How I use to be always lying, being selfish, and manipulating. I am so grateful for my sobriety. I CHOOSE to LIVE. I choose to LIVE. NEVER AGAIN. I've been to HELL and BACK. Heaven is on EARTH. Honey, I love you so much for being my wife. My wife with me.*

This day was to prove to be a wonderful ending to a fantastic weekend. I was starting to spend more and more time with my wife. It was like we were dating all over again, spending a lot of time talking about feelings and caressing her hands. I treasured the time we shared.

Afterwards I went back to my apartment and started watching television. Watching television is not a bottom-line behavior. On the contrary, I watch so little, I don't think twice about it. But in the beginning of my recovery, I didn't have the insight that I have now, so when I watched a program about drugs and drug addicts, I didn't realize I would be triggered with middle-circle thoughts. The program left me feeling really uncomfortable. It had a girl in it to whom I was very attracted, and she was smoking crystal meth. This type of person is exactly the type of girl I would look for while I was in active addiction. In some strange way, I found her being a using addict attractive, alluring, and I was drawn into fantasy. I was thinking how cool it would be to hook up with this girl and started to fantasize about us getting together. This type of thinking is middle-circle behavior. It's definitely a slippery slope for me and could lead me into inner-circle behaviors if I were to obsess long enough about them.

Today I am very mindful of the television programs I watch. The content has to be acceptable. I know what triggers me. I change channels immediately when there are materials that I find objectionable to my viewing. At times I will leave the room if I am at someone else's house. Recovery just doesn't appear; I have to make it happen, one day at a time, sometimes one minute at a time, day by day. The reason: because I'm worth it.

April 4, 2005

Papa, thank you for giving me the wisdom to see myself through another day in sobriety. Yesterday I was confronted with a person who I acted with, then you put someone right in my path who, when I was in active addiction, I would have flirted with. Not anymore. With your wisdom, you have allowed me to come from shame to grace. I love you so much for being there to guide me. It's your "word" that will allow me to sleep guilt free and shame free. I can't say pain free. I make it a point to keep certain memories up front in my mind to constantly remind me of where I was.

Now I'm working on balance, balancing work, myself, working out, Lainie all into one day, one day at a time. Thank you, Papa, for all your love; it does make a difference knowing your there. I love you for that. Goodnight. I'm going to read before I fall asleep. Until tomorrow, your humble servant, me.

With every new day that I arise alive, I truly feel blessed. I have found a new inner strength that I've been able to springboard from each day to the next. Whether I've learned a little nuance about myself or learned something about this great world around me. I use this newfound energy to assist in elevating me internally with the confidence and strength from the day before. What a better gift I do not know. This has helped confirm to me that I am growing emotionally and psychologically. I owe it all to my eternal Father, whom I fondly call Papa, and humbly kneel at His feet as His servant whose will is my calling one day at a time.

April 6, 2005

As I look back, I can't help but to cry as I remember the pain I was in just six short weeks ago and the joy I feel today for the little time of freedom I have as of this moment. Papa, I love you for another day of sobriety. It's really one-fifteen in the morning of April seventh. I'm up with work and reading. I love you, Papa.

In these short beginnings of an uncharted journey, I've found myself becoming emotional at the drop of a thought. In this case, it was an anniversary of six weeks of freedom from the heinous disease that had such a strangle-hold on my life. Tears of joys rushed down my face as I thanked my higher power for his everlasting love and support of my program and myself.

April 8, 2005

Well, another day has blown by, and I've learned another tidbit of wisdom. Yesterday in a meeting, one of my fellows shared what was quite beautiful. He said, "Sex addiction for me was not about sex." I was floored; to come to that realization took a lot of thought. What I noticed was that he was absolutely correct. Sex addiction, for me, is not about sex, either. It was an instrument, a way to isolate, to cover up my deep-seeded feelings of pain, neglect, and the feelings of abandonment etc. It was PAIN. It created SHAME. I hated it. My addiction wanted to suck out the very life I had. It wanted my soul. It wanted all of me. It wanted my life. It preyed upon me. It grew stronger and more cunning as the years progressed. It was sucking out my light, that special gift from God. I love you, Papa, for allowing me to have the clarity to see my way back into your guidance. Allowing me to feel, allowing me to see. I'm so grateful for your love.

I accept your love, I accept who I am, I accept what I am. I embrace what I am. I have the ability to say no to the pain one day at a time. Each day that has passed by has given me the ability to improve upon myself progressively. Thank you, Papa. Your wisdom, your love, and your light light my way. I will forever be your servant available to support your desires for me as I go through my own recovery. From shame to grace, one day at a time.

I never stop being amazed by what I learn as each day progresses, and this day was no exception. At my meeting that night, one of my fellows shared something about himself that totally caught me off-guard. When he stated that sex addiction for him was not about sex, I was stunned. Then I listened closer as he explained himself. He alluded to the fact that as much as it was sex that he engages in, sex in and of itself was not what his addiction was about. It was used as a way to cope with his inner pain.

All of a sudden, a light bulb went off in my head and I smiled and said to myself, "Me, too." What a great insight, I thought. Here I was looking for the answer of where my addiction started when in fact, I realized it was a "why" my addiction started. I smiled again like I just solved the greatest mystery of my time.

Now I was onto something. I could start connecting all the dots of my emotional rollercoaster and clearly see how I too used sex as my coping skill instead of healthy avenues. I now had another tool for my recovery. This was a glorious day and as usual, I thanked the one source for my new enlightenment. Thank you, Papa.

April 9, 2005

"Feeling," something that I have lacked seeing or being with for a very long, long time. Tonight I began to feel sad. Lainie and I were invited to a charity event. I bought tickets. I arrived early, as requested a day earlier by the charity chairwoman. I told Lainie to arrive later— the party started at six at night. Being the punctual person my wife is, she arrived on time at six.

I was taken aback; she looked stunning. She wore a black pant suit with a white-armed shear top. The only word to describe the way she looked was radiant. She had taken so much time to prepare, do make-up, drive over alone, that I'm sure when she decided to leave early, she felt a little slighted that she missed time with me as well. My duties had included selling drink tickets to the incoming guests. I had turned in my bank three times. My feet were sore. I don't drink and I don't gamble and quite honestly, after seeing how beautiful my wife looked and knowing how little time I get to be with her, I started to feel sad that I wasn't with her. She took so much time to be with me. This evening we were to be together, and I had to be a volun-

teer. I understand it was for a good cause, but I felt sad that we were not together, enjoying the show.

In the past in my addiction, I would have taken my wife's leaving as rejection and did the old "fuck you." I would have gone and acted out at the adult bookstore or on the internet. I'm proud to say that I didn't because of you, Papa. With your guidance, I have started to feel. Thank you, Father.

I felt sad, all right. I left early from the event and went to call Lainie to see if she would go out with me even after she wasn't with me during the charity event. I wasn't able to reach her for the rest of the evening. Instead of acting out, I chose to be with my feelings. I went back to the apartment and wrote the passage above. I am very proud of myself; since this time has passed, I have come to be with feelings that were as compelling as the day I felt sad. The difference is over time, by the grace of God to guide me, I have come to understand what feelings feel like and to be able to cope with them as they appear. There is such a special joy that I feel when I come through the other side of a new feeling that I'm just learning about. This is recovery in action. I'm so grateful for my recovery.

April 11, 2005

Once again, Papa, you amaze me with one more day of beauty. It started with feeling good and ended feeling good and very proud as well. I'm very proud because today is the sixth week, fourth day, and twenty-third hour of sobriety. I love you for this, and I'm so tired.

There is nothing more satisfying that a fulfilled day of sobriety.

April 12, 2005

Hmmm...today things are starting to unravel. What I mean is that all of my work is colliding with itself. The shop is behind on getting my work complete, which makes all of the installa-

tions back up. I feel I'm overwhelmed. I'm just going to accept it as it is and not let it affect me. Instead I'm just going to be with my feelings. Thank you, Papa.

"Overwhelm": Transitive verb, state of covering over, upset, overthrow.

This is an interesting feeling that I recognized was happening in me. I started to get antsy, my head started feeling like a press was squeezing it from the sides, I started to sweat around my neck and temples. My brain felt like it was frozen. I couldn't make a move mentally. I felt so useless, and yet I knew I had to make a move to stop the feeling from continuing. What a paradox. On one hand, I feel like I'm mentally paralyzed and on the other hand, I know I have to concentrate really hard and make a decision to move in a direction, any direction. I finally sat down and looked over all of the jobs I had pending, reviewed each install date, and then organized each job by date and time, then I called each customer and explained that their install would be delayed. I was doing the right thing. I was being responsible.

You know, it's a funny thing, this thing called life. One thing I have learned through recovery is that I can make plans, whatever they may be, and God laughs. Time is not an element over which I have any control. Everything is done in His time, whatever that ends up being.

April 13, 2005

After looking at the last two days, I can see a pattern of nothing, just truths of days gone by. Some good, some bad, and some okay. The common denominator is that they all have twenty-four hours. How I handle those twenty-four hours or react to them makes all the difference. Thank you, Papa, for each day. I love you. You are my guiding light.

This was my "great insight" about time and how it connects to each day. I have good days, I have bad days, and I have okay days. The way I react to those hours that make up the days is how

I feel. The best is that I'm never alone throughout any of those twenty-four hours; I have Papa by my side, guiding each and every step I take.

April 14, 2005

Papa, a friend called me last night and asked me to TOAST him and his bride at their wedding this weekend. I was honored. I felt blessed to be a part. He is a man of high moral and ethical conviction. Papa, I'm falling asleep as I write this...I need to go to sleep.

I'll remember this day forever. I couldn't believe that I was asked to do the toast. I have so much respect for this friend. I think of him like a brother. I even told him about my addiction when I first came clean. His reaction was one that floored me. He was extremely supportive and still wanted to be friends. He told me he was proud of me for facing my issues head-on. This show of support made me appreciate him even more. I feel blessed to have a friend like him, "support without judgment."

April 15, 2005

Ty, Papa, for this wonderful day. Yesterday I did my fifth Breathwork session. It was very intense. I reviewed my anger toward my birth mother for letting me go. It was something I held in for forty-three years. After the session, I felt an openness toward others that I never felt before. I felt "lighter" in my being, where an opportunity to have more positive energy entered into my life. I like these feelings; I am so grateful for this growth in my life. I feel like I'm learning about life for the first time. I'm getting in touch with the issues that I've tried to bury for thirty-plus years. I love you, Papa, for all that you have allowed me to learn. I am your humble servant in waiting, now and forever.

Every time I went through a Breathwork session, I felt a sensation in my body, leaving me feeling physically lighter, as if weights had been lifted off my body. This time was no different. Emotionally a new inner confidence came upon me unlike any other time in any other session. It was as if I was given an injection into my soul that acted as a shield over my heart. This type of therapy was a gift. I treasure the gifts it gave to me.

April 18, 2005

It's eleven-twenty at night, and I just finished reading the first thirty days of a journal I had written before I surrendered, wow. A lot of confusion, pain, isolation, delusion, and doubt. I couldn't help but to feel bad for the person I used to be. Time has passed since those days were written. My mind and soul have gained a new perspective on life. I know this is just the beginning of my journey, but it's a healthy journey.

Robin, my stepdaughter, may have her views about me; she owns them. Her opinions are her own. They can't hurt me. In time, if she gives me the time in her heart and mind, then she may come to understand me from a different perspective. I'm not holding out. I know she only cares about her mom—me too, just differently. I know she has seen me hurt her mother very badly. I'm responsible.

As I read the pages of the journal I had written before I surrendered, I couldn't help but feel pity for the previous life I led. It was filled with loneliness, delusion, and pain. How I managed to stay alive and function is amazing in of itself. The delusions really scared me when I read them again. I really truly felt that I was doomed to live a life as a transvestite and die by either an overdose or AIDS. The entries would have made even the best professionals scratch their heads. I was really scared when I read them.

April 19, 2005

It was eleven-fifteen at night, and the phone rang. I was almost asleep. It was a fellow SAA member, Scott. He had left his wife tonight. He was scared and felt alone. I can only Thank you,

*Papa, for giving me your wisdom and being available to sup-
port those who are in need of support as they go through their
own growth. I am your humble servant. Scott and I spoke until
one-fifteen in the morning.*

While back when I was using the online SLAA meeting, I had
met a fellow who sent me a quote that goes something like this:
"When the hand of recovery reaches out, it's my responsibility to
support that person." I may have forgotten its exact wording, but
the idea will never leave me. I remember those first days when I
was in recovery, so many questions, so afraid at times to make a
move at all. My sponsor was the one I would call. Today I call
members in the fellowship as my support network has grown
over the years. By the grace of God, support is as close as a phone
call.

Scott was very upset. I completely understand where he was
coming from. I went through the same situation myself only
three months earlier in January 2005. I understood the feelings
Scott was experiencing. One thing recovery does is it allows
people to chat about issues someone has gone through at one
point or another, a brother helping a brother. Since recovery is the
most important aspect of my life, if the phone rings, I don't care
at what time; I will answer it. If it's late my feeling is if it's important to that brother, then it's important for me to listen, too.

This program has been the saving grace for my life, and when
someone calls, it's God will for me to reach out and assist the
brother in need. Thank you, Papa.

April 20, 2009

*It's eleven-forty-five at night. It seems as though this is my time
to write lately; it's okay. I feel good about writing. I like
knowing I have a past to review and see growth from. I was
reading my journal while I was in addiction, and I felt sad for
myself as I was, not "poor me" or "victim," just sad. I felt the
pain, I saw the isolation, and I sensed the despair. I read the
ideas regarding suicide. Reviewing these notes gave me a real*

sense of gratitude for where I am today. I'm so blessed. Thank you, Papa.

I am so grateful for the pages in my journal while I was in addiction. One would think this material should be torn up and thrown away. Not me. I'm grateful. In recovery there is a passage called the "Promises," which we read at every meeting. In it one line talks about the past and how as addicts we should never shut the door on it or ignore it. This is for a very good reason. The past is like a painting; it shows our true colors, which light the path of our existence. For this reason, we can easily want to forget where we've been or done. It is, however, an integral part of recovery. By never shutting the door on the past or ignoring it, we allow ourselves to heal by acknowledging our growth from where we used to be to where we are now. If I were to forget where I've been, it's safe to assume I'd be right back into my addiction. A place I hope to God I never have to experience again.

April 22, 2005

Hello, Papa. It's been a very funny day, not ha- ha funny, funny as in irregular. I know you test me on a daily basis, and I know you do not have any designs to harm me. I also know that I have no control over other people or events that are controlled by other people as well. Additionally, I know with the wisdom I've learned from you, it's how I react to events or people that lead to my feelings.

I really don't have anything else to add regarding this day. The short, concise words it say it all.

April 23, 2005

Tonight is the first night of Passover. I am alone this year. No family, no friends. A chance to reflect. A consequence of my addiction; I'm not going to beat myself up. I know the past acts of my addiction had caused the pain of those close to me, those who choose not to have contact with me now. Robin, for one.

It's okay, I'm not mad at her. On the contrary, I'm glad she is there to be with Lainie. I can't expect Robin to rationally accept my acts or addiction. She will either in time come to understand and forgive or she won't. Either way I'm not going to stop my recovery.

As I know, NO ONE or ANY EVENT can make me go back to my addiction. I miss not being there with everyone this evening. I'm going to work out and focus on my recovery. I love you, Papa. I feel sad. It's okay, I'm glad I'm alive to be here to feel sad. I love you, Papa. It's nine o'clock in the evening, and I just saw an article in the newspaper on PASSOVER and it struck me that I too was in slavery. The PHAROAH was my addiction. He forced me to serve his desires as he chose. If I tried to escape, I was tortured with SHAME and GUILT until I submitted back to his will.

I would pray to GOD to take me out of bondage or take me off this planet. Then one night GOD promised me DELIVERANCE. It was February 24, 2005, at nine-fifteen at night. He spoke to me, crystal clear. I was told to wake up from a sleep state. My thoughts were brought into focus. I was clear of my words I thought and spoke. I was being cradled with warmth in both my mind and heart. I knew who it was. It was He, the one I call God, the one I call Papa. He was with me. I knew I was safe. He parted the waters between good and evil and told me to walk through the two ideals and save my life. This was my chance at living. In a split second, I knew it was my choice between living and dying. I chose life and at that moment turned my will over to Him after acknowledging that I was indeed a sex addict.

As Moses acknowledged his belief in only one God and like the Ten Commandments he was given. I too after my acknowledgement was given my commandments; those were the twelve steps. The most important of all was this the humility I have experienced under His guidance, learning his ways, following his guidance, serving His ideals, one day at a time. Thank you, Papa.

On this night, I asked a very simple question: "Why am I alone?" This was a very sad night for me and a time to rejoice as well. I knew I physically was alone, but I knew I was safe in my higher power's arms. I was being cradled with love and warmth. I sat in my room and started reading the newspaper in bed when I noticed an article about Passover. I began to reflect upon my life. Suddenly the parallels started to circulate in my head. The message started to become extremely clear; in the past I too was enslaved, living in bondage. As the message settled into my conscious mind, I started to write feverishly in my journal.

That was then and today, I draw from the insight of that special day. It's no coincidence that the title of this book is *Out of Bondage,* for I too was delivered from evil and brought into His glory, just like the tens of thousands of Hebrews back in Pharaoh's regime. I also learned to listen carefully to His words of guidance as my teacher. On this day I wrote, "No one or any event can make me go back to my addiction." Unfortunately, I had no crystal ball to look into my future. A RELAPSE was no exception. God showed me what a relapse was so I'd understand that I always need to be on my guard and that anyone or any event may in fact BE the cause of such a slip. Believe me, going through a relapse is a part of the process of recovery, but it doesn't have to be the common denominator to everyone's recovery.

April 24, 2005

In my heart, I feel the notion for God's will for me. I am to be a voice for victims of sexual abuse and of sexual addiction. Telling my story, sharing my story, for others to understand that it's not their fault. They can have a life. A healthy, productive life. They have to want it. I know I wanted it. God led me to it. Papa, you opened my eyes, mind, and heart to it. "It" is a happy life, where deceit and torture are no longer the staples of the day. Rather love, support, and honor each hour one day at a time. Ty (Thank you), Papa. I love you.

I'm a firm believer there are no coincidences in life, truly none. I believe our whole life is mapped out for us and we just live it out with few variances. Like my divine intervention, I was spoken to in a dream where I was told to write this book. I believe that conversation was divine as well. So these sentences I know in my heart and soul are part of my destiny. I believe it is God's will for me. I also believe its God's will for you to be reading these words right now.

When I wrote this day's entry into my journal, I never thought it would be a book I would be writing to share my story, hoping that I'm able to make a difference in someone else's life. This is God's will for me, and I do not waver from his request. I know it's what I'm supposed to be doing in my life. If I can assist just one person and make him or her feel a part of humanity verses feeling alone, then I've done my work. My hope is that it reaches more. Thank you, Papa.

April 27, 2005

I found Dan from group; he called me today. He let me know he was okay. Last Saturday he tried to commit suicide and failed. He was Baker Acted. I'm glad. More on how I feel about his attempt later.

It's not a joke that people die from this disease. I learned several things in my first weeks of recovery. Besides the fact that it's cunning, baffling, and powerful, there's no cure, it's progressive, and it doesn't give a rat's ass if it kills you. I never knew anyone who actually died from it, but I didn't have to wait long before I heard about one guy who killed himself and left a letter saying he couldn't take the shame any longer. Him I understood; I was so low I thought about same thing on more than one occasion. First there was this guy who used to be in group with my old therapist. He was the one who told us about this guy. The next guy was someone in my own men's group. He acted out really badly and was so shameful and guilty. He took a knife to his throat and just missed his jugular vein. When I went to the hospital to visit him, he had staples running the full length of his six-inch slash. It really blew me away. Here I was, face to face with someone who felt so shameful regarding his issues that he chose to end his life. I felt sick to my stomach after seeing his neck and really grateful for my sobriety. It was a real rude awakening. I could have been him and succeeded. Papa, I'm so grateful for your love.

April 29, 2005

Papa, I'm writing tonight after having a great day of just being with the ups and downs of the day. A normal day in the course of life. For me, it was a "great day" as I faced all of the challenges head on and did not try to hide out from my feelings. Early this morning, I got a call from one of my employees, who tried to use guilt on me regarding her work habits, saying she was just doing the best she could. I didn't mention anything about the effort she put in; I was upset at her attitude. I let her know that, and she tried to turn the tide on me making me "bad and wrong." I will not respond to that type of game. Thank you, Papa, for the wisdom I have learned from you regarding patience. Goodnight.

One thing I've been learning on my journey is how to be in the moment with my feelings as they occur. Sometimes I react negatively to them, in which case I use them as learning experiences. But for the most part, I've been having positive results. On this day, it started with one of my employees giving me an excuse for her work habits and trying to make me the bad guy.

In the book written by Eric Burne, M.D., *Games People Play*, it discusses the subconscious psychological games people use on a daily basis. My employee was playing one of the games described in the book. Thank God for recovery because as I was living in the present moment, I was conscious enough to not buy in to her game. I did not react negatively. I chose to act very business-like and directed her to a positive resolution. I recommend this book because it educates and describes the basic states of mind as addicts we adopt while in our addiction and how it relates to our recovery. It's outdated material, for the most part, but is clear and concise with its methods. Personally, I think it should be a required reading for parents and high school students.

I am once again moving to the grooving of the day, taking in all the bad and good as it showed up. This is what recovery has taught me. "Living life on life's terms" is a favorite recovery slogan. It's so great. It says so much in a little sentence. As an addict, I wouldn't live life on life's terms if it was put in front of me with a bow wrapped around it. My M.O. was to run, hide, isolate, or do anything to escape having to deal with reality in the moment. I was famous for my excuses, stories, or lies as long as I could get out of the present. Living life on life's terms required effort, something I was just not willing to do before I got into recovery.

Today I feel so blessed to be able to be present to accept life's challenges as they appear. I've matured and I see it. I no longer feel as though I'm only thirteen years old emotionally. I know I've matured closer to my true age, but I know I still have a ways to go. I have to say I'm very happy with the progress I've made so far, one day at a time. Ty, Papa.

April 30, 2005

> *"Recovery is an action that takes courage to face."*
> *L.J. Schwartz*

It takes a strong hand to say no to temptation, as an addict knows. I am one. I am one in recovery. I look back at the last sixty days plus and am proud to say that I've arrived at this spot. I know it is just a tiny fragment of recovery—recovery, nonetheless. It pains me to know the actions of my addiction created the horror and nightmares of my wife's world. I own my actions; I'm accountable for my future actions. I know I can't take away the pain of her memories. I will not lie to her. I will not hide out. I also know I will not obsess over the past. I know I will not have control if Lainie obsesses over the past. I understand she alone can either own it or let it go. I love you, Papa. Thank you for your love. I understand that I have hurt her. I understand that I have to allow her the time to vent at me. I will apologize to her tomorrow for not allowing her to feel her pain. Ty, Papa, for allowing me to see the truth of your teachings.

The truth of my wreckage lives. I know I am responsible for it. In recovery I am learning how to handle situations that used to baffle me. I make it a point to be proactive with issues before they arise. One tool I created for myself deals with woman who smoke and driving. As an addict, I've mentioned before that I have an incredible fetish for females who smoke. This would not be a problem if I wasn't a sex addict, but I am, so it is a big issue, especially when I'm driving.

Let me explain. I live in South Florida, so air conditioning is pretty standard in cars. But if a smoker is driving, generally he or she will crack their windows to let out the secondhand smoke. I happen to know this from thirty years of smoking experience. So as I drive the road, I would actively look for cracked windows on cars. If I found one I would speed up, slow down, change lanes, or whatever it took to catch a glimpse of the driver smoking. Generally I'd notice if it was a female or male right away. If it was male I would stop following, but if it was female I would go into a sort of trance-like state where time and space would seemingly stand still.

At this point, I would position myself in my car such that I could watch the girl or woman go through her ritual of smoking. My fantasies would start and rapidly grow to the point where I would say to myself, "That's right, baby, suck on that cigarette," or "Mmm—you like that, don't you?" The fantasies would grow so intricate and deep that I would start shouting, "That's right, baby, suck it good!" This ritual for me even took me to a place where I would motion to the person that I liked what I saw as she smoked. I was out of control at this point. All reality at this point was what I thought in my mind. Warped as it was, I would think that if a woman was smoking, then she was an "oral satisfaction machine" and was put on this earth to satisfy men orally. There was no question in my mind of this act. As a transvestite, "we" girls needed to stick together. All this from seeing a window rolled down an inch or two in a car.

In my first sixty days I came to realize that these thoughts and actions were out of control. What I couldn't believe was that I actually thought it was okay to carry on like this in the past. I also saw how the wreckage of my path was shared by those I cared for as well. But I couldn't control how Lainie handled her reaction to my wreckage. I knew I had done it, I was accountable for it, and in the future I would be responsible for my actions, but I had to let go of it. I had to keep the memories close enough to keep in my mind but far enough away that they didn't interfere with my daily living. This was important so as not to forget where I've come from. This was where my recovery had taken me so far, and I was extremely grateful.

May 1, 2005

Another day passed, one day at a time. It's seven before twelve midnight. I'm very grateful, Papa, for this day to be alive. I went and visited a friend who is in a psych ward after he tried killing himself. This disease is powerful, cunning, and baffling. It doesn't care that I want to live; it wants me back. I feel it rear its fangs to attack back into me. But knowing what I know today, I have tools to turn away from its lust for my soul. Papa, thank you for your guidance. I'm crying tears of joy as I write this, knowing without your love I would not be here.

I met a woman online who was a videographer of smoking-fetish pornography. We spoke about my desires of becoming a smoking-fetish coke whore and wanting to be in porn as a career. She hadn't met an attractive transvestite to date and was up for the challenge. I told her I wanted to do a real nasty "gang bang" video. I wanted to be totally dressed to the nines, full make-up, wig, my five-inch heels and, of course, smoking my long one-twenty cigarettes as I was repeatedly ravaged by men. She said she could definitely get me cocaine to totally fulfill my requests. She was so hot on the idea that we spoke almost daily either by phone or email. I thought she was the best contact I had ever made. Finally a woman who understood my desires to be a prostitute, my smoking fetish, and didn't mind if I supported her with revenue from my "tricks." She didn't even mind if I did coke. I thought I had finally met the woman of my dreams. What I now know is she was my ticket to hell. She represented every nuance of my addiction, from the drugs, videos, illicit sexual encounters, to my supporting her financially. I now know I was on my way to my grave.

After looking back, once I declared my addiction, the realization of who this woman was became crystal clear. She was my addiction's "princess of death" here on earth. She was enabling me to commit suicide. I am clear that the month of April 2005 I planned on killing myself. I was days away from buying my airline tickets. I had already isolated myself from my family and friends. I only needed to make the pornography.

In the book Out of the Shadows, *by Patrick Carnes, Ph.D., he talks about how our addiction keeps us set up in a belief system that is a vacuum of shame. He states on page 108, "That feelings of inadequacy and failure predominate. Addicts even see humiliation and degradation as justified or deserved." For me, this meant that all I was setting myself up for with this woman in New York I deserved and I was justified in doing. My thinking had become so impaired, it seemed normal for me to become a smoking-fetish coke whore, even if it meant leaving everyone and everything behind. Then the real clarity of "waking up" after I had done all the coke and porn would have shamed me so badly that suicide would have been my ONLY option. The pain from the shame would have sent me over the edge. I was finished living life as I knew it. No one would have wanted me any longer, not anyone who counted, that is…Lainie, my friends, anyone. Death was my only option. So today I'm alive and grateful for it, grateful for my recovery and grateful that I'm able to write about it. I love you, Papa. Goodnight.*

I remember this day very vividly. As I saw my friend Dan, I was horrified at the staples that lined his wound. He really wanted out. He wanted to say goodbye. I understand his pain. I remember how close I came to actually wanting to kill myself. This disease really doesn't care who you are. It wants your soul. It feeds off of healthy souls to grow; that's what recovery has illuminated in my heart and mind, *the truth.*

As I look back at this day, I can't help but to be incredibly grateful for God's intervention with me. Without Him or His love, I would have surely perished. The woman I had met clearly wasn't a friend; rather she was from the darkest bowels of hell, ready to enable me to my demise. I can tell you this…if you let this addiction have its way, none of these words I've typed can help you. Only God can save you at this point. May you find Him now.

May 2, 2005

I love you, Papa. It's eleven-fifteen in the evening. I just finished at the gym. I thank you for your grace to have allowed me to have another free from my addiction. I'm starting the "steps" of my program.

I left my BNI group today. It has become apparent to me that ALL my commitments need to be centered on my recovery first, then on me. Then when I'm able to after my business is in a stable place, I can think about giving a commitment as large as BNI another opportunity.

In addition to going to my SAA meetings on a weekly basis, I also started a workout regiment at a local gym. This was to assist in creating consistency in my life that I so dearly needed. My life ran a hundred miles an hour without any real rhyme or reason to it and daily consistency didn't exist, until now. Four meetings a week and working out two days on, one day off every week. I even started eating at certain defined hours and making sure I went to bed at a consistent time as well.

There was one constant I did have in my life, and that was Business Network International (BNI), a national network of local chaptered business groups. We met every week on a Tuesday morning at seven. They are a rigorous business group that requires a great commitment. What I noticed was that my time with this group was not personally productive time. In other words, it was expendable. Since I entered recovery and saw how much of a commitment it was going to take on my part than anything else other than actually working, working out, eating, or sleeping was expendable. I wasn't playing Russian roulette with my life any longer. I knew I had to make adjustments to my priorities. BNI was out.

May 3, 2005

What a morning...it was beautiful morning, sunny and breezy. At nine in the morning, I got a call from my buddy, Dan, a member of my men's group who attempted suicide. He asked me if I would assist him. He was being discharged from the hospital today and asked if I would give him some moral support by coming over to his house for a couple of hours.

Papa, thank you, thank you for getting me to assist in your will for me. Kari just said the other day, "When one door closes, another door opens." Well, she was right. I look back a week ago, and I was concerned about leaving my business group. I know that my priorities have changed since I got into recovery. My first priority is recovery, my second priority is me, and my third priority is my business. Then comes my business group. What I noticed was my business group was a very large commitment, so much so that it was taking away time from my recovery and business. I feel that my decision to let that commitment go opened up a newfound timeframe to assist in my recovery and my business. Thank you, Papa.

I have to say I didn't exactly feel comfortable giving Dan the support he requested, but I did it without question. The discomfort I remember was surrounding the scene of the suicide. There was still blood all over the floor in the bathroom, and the staples in his neck made me feel sick.

I had empathy for Dan. I knew in my heart it was the right place for me to be. It's what God wanted me to do. I knew he appreciated it as well. Dan also asked me to accompany him to the video store where he rented the videos to which he had acted out. I told him sure. After a while, my discomfort subsided and it was just Dan as usual, quite, reserved, and apologetic. I assured him more than once that there was no reason for him to apologize to me. What he went through was a traumatic event, and I was okay with supporting him. I told him about my BNI group and how the time I was spending with him was exactly what God had led me to do, shifting my priorities with recovery and family versus business and dollars. I was honored he called me, feeling secure enough to be comfortable with me around him. The time we spent soon passed by, and I was once again in my car driving home, feeling very blessed I was able to assist a brother in need. Thank you, Papa.

May 6, 2005

It's one-fifteen in the morning. I know it's been a long day, but it has been very productive as well. For the first time in my life as an adult, I'm starting to see the fruits of my "labor." The labor is my recovery. I understand how important it is to be honest with myself and my commitment to keep my recovery the first and respected priority from the moment I awaken in the morning. Papa, I see how you truly do love me. I see your signs of life all around me. The pearls of wisdom while not speaking. The prosperity I'm earning without your "money." All from your love alone and, of course, your helpers. Ty, Papa. I love you.

This day really spells out the level of commitment I shifted to in order to survive. What I recognized was that there was no greater commitment I could make for myself. I never had made such a choice in my life. I was growing, I was maturing, and it's clear in my entry how dedicated I had become. I chose to live, I chose life; with that comes responsibilities I was starting to accept as an adult, one day at a time.

May 6, 2005

It's six-fifteen in the morning, and I am up and looking forward to a beautiful day. In this moment, however, I am grateful for my recovery and the wonderful things it has brought to me. I never thought I would be here to see how simple quiet time could be. How enjoyable to be in this moment with you, Papa. Ty for all your love for me. Today I will continue to work on my recovery and reach out toward others, cre-

ating support for me. I love you. This is what I achieved thus far. The ability to appreciate life at its simplest level of being or better stated to appreciate my being in life as its being created in the moment. Ty. I love you for getting me to slow down enough inside and outside. I'm learning. Recovery has given me this ability. You have shown me love, and I will follow your will as you alone restore me to sanity.

Recognizing that it was God's will for me to slow down, I began to hear Him speak to me. I was also enjoying how the little things in life were coming into view, from the beauty of seeing an osprey flying overhead to witnessing the magic of a sunset with an orangey-red sky. I was learning that my time spent in recovery and supporting others in recovery had a much richer effect on my life than all the money I may have ever owned. Thank you, Papa. I am very grateful for your guidance.

May 9, 2005

Papa, thank you for this day of deliverance from my addiction. Being in recovery has given me more joy and happiness, strength, and insight than I ever knew before. Today I can say I've made the right decision to leave my business group and place more commitment on my recovery. What showed up for me was that I now have placed the emphasis on assisting myself as opposed to others.

For years while wearing a "face" of contentment, I've made it a point to help others succeed while I suffered in pain, in isolation. Not any longer do I suffer in pain or isolation. I have freed myself with God's help. I've humbly turned my will over to God in order to gain His will for me. I know, Papa, that you gave me the strength to make the right choice to put myself on top. I finally took the time to see there was no one who was going to give a shit about me except me. I've spent years helping others get ahead all the while being in pain. Now I only see myself as the person to help. I'm not in pain, I'm in recovery. The pain no longer hides behind the mask of deceit; rather it stands alone only in the memories of what was and no longer is. Papa, you saved your son, and I've turned my will and life over to you to support others looking for the hand of recovery, your love, your warmth, and your wisdom. Ty, Papa. I hope that as my tomorrows arrive that others see the truth in recovery.

Tomorrow is my father's birthday. I miss him. I also spoke to Lainie about moving out of my apartment. She asked if I would consider moving back into the house. I hesitated to say yes because I'm not ready yet. To know this is okay. I'm being honest with myself. It's better for the both of us. I want the hand of recovery to be strong as it grips a relationship of love to hold tight and firm. To make sure I don't let go. I love her. I'm not willing to have any pain hurt her again. Now I'm ready to start my step work. I feel this will give me the foundation I'm looking for before I feel strong enough to go home. I love you. Papa.

After taking a couple of days to let my decision to leave my business group sink in, I came to realize just how right the choice turned out to be. I finally was putting myself and my own personal success ahead of everything else. I know this sounds selfish. But if I hadn't taken a stand to put my recovery ahead of everyone and everything, then chances are I wouldn't be here typing these pages.

The decision to place one's own wellness above all else shows the most honorable desire for personal growth. There is a quote that we all recite at the end of our meetings that is the true message of the recovery work we all share: "It works if you work it, so work it; you're worth it." This directly corresponds to the level of commitment we each choose to live with our recovery. As statistics have shown in the past, this twelve-step program, as simple as it is, works if you have the courage and perseverance to pursue it. This is a promise many before me have lived by. And after all, you are worth it. So when the hand of recovery reaches out to me, I have a responsibility to assist, and that is God's will for me.

May 10, 2005

Pop, it's your birthday. I'm sad. I miss you. I'm mad at you as well. Why didn't you make provisions for me for the future that

I would have known about? Did you really not love me? Was it all a sham? Regardless, I believed you loved me. Now I'm going to learn how to create balance in my life. I know I will always be provided for by you, Papa. I have and am learning to submit my total will over to you for all of my ways, not just for my recovery. I feel in my heart that as your son, I have a purpose here, and I promise to you I will let go of my work and focus more on your work for me. I will. Ty, Papa. I am your humble servant.

This was a very emotional day for me. I was at a stoplight in Downtown Ft. Lauderdale and just thinking about my father, and I started to grieve and cry. I missed him. It's funny to say, Lainie and I have discussed this before and came to the conclusion that the greatest gift my father gave me was nothing because it forced me to become self-reliant. His death also was the catalyst that started my downward spiral to hell. The pain I went through and subsequently my acting out daily in order to medicate myself I look at as another gift he gave me. Without his passing, I doubt I would have been brought to recovery. Pop, I love you and miss you and dedicate this book to you as well. Without you I would not be here today.

May 11, 2005

Yesterday, as I was feeling my father's birthday go by, I grieved his memory. I'm not sure I grieved a whole lot when he passed. As I sat in my truck at a red light, I thought about him, his smile, his walk. I heard his voice, the way he chuckled. I felt him near me as I looked at his picture on my dash. It was one o'clock in the afternoon. I just started to cry. I said to his picture, "I miss you. I really miss you." I waited for him to tell me it was okay. The picture just stared back at me, and I realized again he was truly gone. Pop, I miss you so much. I'm not all alone like I thought I was when you first left me, but you were a great joy in my life and I truly miss you.

You never knew I was a sex addict. I know after you passed you saw me in my pain. I know you were able to see me act out, the activities, the places, the lies, and the pain. It was hard on me to lose you. I couldn't and wouldn't believe it was true. All I felt was the emptiness of your love. You were my one, my only tether to unconditional love, so I thought. I hurt so badly. I just wanted to be with you. I didn't care about anything else. I was numb to everyone, my friends, my work started sliding; it was awful. My addiction kept me from seeing the truth of how to feel your loss. Since my sobriety, I have been able to grieve. I also know there are others in my life who love me like you did and more. I know in my heart you're with me always, and I know I made you proud. Now I'm working on me and making myself proud of me. I love you, Pop. I'll always remember your love for me. Thanks to my sobriety, I feel joy. Thanks to God, I found love again.

Love, that feeling that bonds us together. I'm glad I have the chance to feel it. Sobriety brought this feeling back into my life. Sobriety has allowed me to grieve the death of my father. When my father had died, I was active in my addiction; I was numb to any real feelings. This made me angry. I was getting angry over everything. It didn't matter who was doing what. I was so deep in my addiction and had so much shame that even if you offered me a million dollars to stop acting out, the compulsion was too great.

In contrast, through my sobriety, I had hit a chord that was so buried, it made me cry. I was finally grieving my father's loss. It was a beautiful moment, a celebration of joy. I recognized my growth in this area and was very grateful to my higher power for this new awareness I was witnessing. Additionally, I had come to terms with the emotions I had wrestled with regarding my wife's love for me. Papa, thank you for opening my eyes to the truth.

For such a long time, I kept my wife at arm's length, never allowing her to completely love me. The feelings of being unworthy played over and over in my mind, disallowing any attempt of her love to penetrate my heart. This flaw in my thinking was the catalyst for my acting out. "Why should I care? She can't love the true me." Thankfully, today I know very different. I know my wife's love for me is unconditional, pure of heart and just plain wonderful. God has allowed me, through his guidance, in my life. Pure love, the kind you hear about but usually don't see. This has been the miracle that I have received through this program of sobriety. The same miracle I wish for every addict who finds recovery.

May 13, 2005

Papa, without your guidance, love, and support, I am aware that I would be dead right now. Today at the gym, I met this guy who is working out with a guy I know who is a realtor. I immediately pulled out one of my cards and asked him to give it to his realtor buddy and to let him know I was the guy who was trying to get a hold of him a few weeks back. I then asked this guy what he did for a living. His answer shocked me—I wasn't expecting it.

He informed me that he was an escort, stripper, and porn star who made transsexual porn movies. "So close and yet so far." For a millisecond, I wanted to go back into my addiction. Actually, my addict wanted me to go back for a lifetime. Cunning, baffling, and powerful. I'll write some more tomorrow. I'm falling asleep while I'm writing. I love you, Papa. You are my guiding light.

This day sure threw me for a loop, but I was being guided by a power greater than myself, so I wasn't in any danger. This is how I felt. I knew God was watching over me. He knew what He was doing, I didn't question His thoughts. I just followed along and kept doing the next right thing I knew how to do.

This guy who I met who was the porn star was very confident in who he was, I could tell. I think down deep inside he was sad, though. This is a just a feeling I got after speaking to him for about six months at the gym. The first time I met him, my addiction wanted to jump at the opportunity to find out how to get involved in the porn industry. However, with God by my side, I was able to stay in my adult mode and not allow my inner child to speak for me. I didn't respect this guy, but I didn't judge him. His lifestyle choice was his own and in no way where I wanted to be. I felt sad for him, knowing that as a porn star his opinion of himself and his self-worth were low at best. God wanted me to know this person for me to see what I was looking at for myself. He wanted me to see how I would turn out. Papa, I love you so much for the guidance you have bestowed upon me. Keeping me clear from harm by allowing me to see my future without leaving the present.

May 14, 2005

They say, "they" being recovering addicts, that if we stick to a simple program, "we will be amazed before we are halfway through." Amazed at what? To me the amazing part talks about the miraculous events and clarity I see as I look back at my eighty days in recovery. Papa, I owe my life to your love and guidance. I turned my will over to you and believe that you can help restore me to sanity. Today I know the truth of how submitting my will over can be a miracle in the making. It makes me wonder with all this newfound insight why anyone, including myself, would want to continue on a self-destructive trip.

It was as if I had pricked my finger and then put it in a tank of sharks expecting no reaction from the sharks. Why does my addiction love to fill me full of delusion? Because it can, because it doesn't care about me. It is selfish.

It's three in the morning on Sunday, and I just woke up from a nightmare. It was my addiction. I thought the dreams would go away, but I see I will have to deal with them from time to time. The dream was about drug use. My brother was in it as well as my mother. My brother and I were doing coke when I realized I broke my sobriety. My brother wanted me to continue and keep getting high. I said, "No, I don't want to lose my sobriety." Maybe I didn't. Then I woke up and realized where I was. I was in Walt Disney World with Lainie and never lost my sobriety. I was safe. It was a miracle she was lying next to me. Papa, I am so grateful for your guidance. You lead me out of TEMPTATION. I love you.

Eighty days, one day at a time. I never felt better in my life. I was moving along nicely in my recovery, work was never busier, and most importantly, I was alive. Then the nightmare occurred. I was scared out of my wits. I understand I have no control over my subconscious mind, but when I dream, it's so real. This night was no different. I woke up in a sweat, thinking I had broken my sobriety. Fortunately, it was only a dream. I was so relieved. I thanked my higher power at least a dozen times for keeping me safe. In the recovery rooms, I have heard that dreaming dreams about addiction, whether its drugs, alcohol, or sex, is a common occurrence with addicts and just means that our subconscious mind is running overtime and really can't hurt us. I know from my own experience that these dreams seem so real that as I mentioned earlier, I awaken in a sweat, grateful that I'm still in sobriety.

May 16, 2005

Today, I have to say, was a very nice day. I was able to use the tools I learned from my recovery. I was confronted with a lot of stress from my work. However, insight gave way to the conclusion that the root of stress was due to a lack of communication. Instead of acting out like I would have before, I started reciting the "Serenity Prayer" and can "change" the outcome of the present with a lesson from the past. Papa, I love you for the wisdom I have learned through your guidance.

Another day of recovery, one day at a time.

May 19, 2005

I haven't written for a few days, I've been in my head about a lot of things. Kari's thoughts were that that was the only place I could be since things were bubbling over emotionally for me. I did a Breathwork session at three in the afternoon. It's now five o'clock in the early evening, and I'm mentally and physically tired. I wanted to write, so here I am. I started to write back on the thirteenth about this guy, Gio, whom I met. He was the escort-slash-stripper-slash-porn star. For a split second, my addiction tried to rear its ugly head. Fortunately for me, I had a loved one close by. Thank you, Papa. Papa, it's sad to see how a person who says without hesitation how cool he was for being a porn star seemed very alone to me. He seemed to be very troubled in his face. As he chatted about his prideful events, I felt sadness and pity for him; he seemed so alone. It reminded me of me when I was in active addiction. Thank you, Papa, for letting me see myself as I am now and how happy I am knowing I've broken the chains that used to bind me. I humbly live my life on my knees, thanking you for your love and support. Your ever-faithful servant.

I am so grateful for the time I spent with Gio. My higher power knew exactly what He was doing when He placed me in connection with him. I felt as though I was looking at a mirror reflection of how my life was to be.

Over a six-month period of seeing Gio at the gym, he had confided in me about his on-and-off "relationships" with this female or that transsexual. He would bring these people to the gym to work out, more or less looking for approval. You would have thought there was a revolving door at this guy's house the way he changed girlfriends. Most of the time he would ask my opinion of each new girl he'd bring in and then tell me this one was a stripper or this one was a co-star in his movies. Then a week or so would go by, and he come to the club in a bad mood and you could tell he was on the out with his latest fling. "No one understands me," he would say. "A girl's got to understand I am in the sex trade and know that I'm not choosing between my work or her." That statement reminded me of how narrow-minded I was thinking when I would say to my wife, "If I can't have sex with other people, then you don't love me." Right, and elephants fly, too.

Additionally, this guy had tattoos all over his body. Now don't get me wrong, I like tattoos, but it's been said that people who go way overboard like this person generally have a poor self-image and low self-esteem. What I'm most grateful for is the guidance I was given, allowing me to see what a person who does prostitute himself is like. God wouldn't have placed Gio in my life for any other reason, I'm sure, than to show me where the life of ill repute would lead. For a second, when he said he did transsexual videos, I have to be honest and say I had a flash of glamour fly through my brain. Of course, my addiction always says that.

May 20, 2005

Papa, as I kneel in your presence, I am humbled by new insights of self. I am slowing down my pace and have learned to be more open with my feelings. I did another Breathwork session yesterday and purged some really deep pain that I have been avoiding for many years. This release has allowed more available space for your positive light to flow into me. This new light enlightens my heart and soul with a new warmth and again validates your presence in my life.

I am grateful for your love and guidance. I feel less troubled about my work and its direction. I feel more at peace with myself and more alive with others, being authentic and present in others' presence. More and more of my day is spent grounded and present to each passing moment. Fears and worries have shed their abilities to attach themselves to me. Again, I am humbled by my new education and feel more confident. I love you, Papa. Thank you for taking your time with me.

I wish I was somehow able to give my experience of Breathwork to others. I can only share what has transpired after each session. God knows this therapy has left monumental marks on my life. I truly believe it has been the catalyst for allowing recovery to embed itself so deeply in my soul. After each session, my body, or "vessel," is open to a richer source of positive "God light." These sessions enable my soul to purge out the negative energy of pain that has been stored for many, many, many years on a cellular level. The one I have to thank is the facilitator of these sessions because without her work, I wouldn't have made any strides. Wherever you are, whatever you're doing, thank you.

Then, of course, I have to thank you, Papa, for bringing this person into my life.

May 23, 2005

Papa, I'm moving forward on my own. This morning I had an appointment with a therapist, John. He is the one who had issues with Kari and the Breathwork I'm doing. I listened to his opinions and thanked him for his time, then I left. It was nine in the morning.

I feel that I have come to an important part in my life. Instead of getting angry regarding John's conversations about my Breathwork, I just listened. The waters inside are running very calm. That allows me to feel without reacting, to hear without drifting off, and to pay attention to what is being said. Most importantly, hearing the inner voice inside of me and knowing its truth.

Later on I went to see my business consultants and requested to cancel my contract with their firm. My ideas and ideals for my company have changed, and I'm clear about my new decisions. Papa, without your love, wisdom, and guidance, I would never have been able to make these or any decisions. TyF.

It's amazing what the human mind recalls. This day I can recall as if it was yesterday. I remember so vividly my speaking to John regarding Kari and the fact that she was my facilitator for my Breathwork sessions as well as my roommate. He was not in favor of this arrangement. I appreciate his position and his opinion, but it was my time to take a stand for my own well-being. I had been in therapy for over two years and had been in active recovery for four months. As far as I was concerned, God would not have given me the ability to make a rational decision if He didn't want me to actually do it. So for me, my decision to continue my Breathwork sessions while I was technically still a roommate had no ill effects on me or my emotional stability. Additionally, Kari facilitated with the utmost professionalism. I never felt her crossing any boundaries, at any time, ever.

On the other hand, I had to deal with two people who were my business consultants. As I grew stronger and my ideas and ideals regarding my company changed, so did the need for any further consulting. But these two guys couldn't understand why I was firing them. They just couldn't accept "no."

I felt really good about my two decisions I made this day and know I was following the path my higher power had set before me to take. Papa, I thank you for all your guidance and support and know that no matter what, no one is greater than you. You help me set two new boundaries that day, boundaries that help shape my future. I love you.

May 24, 2005

Thank you, Papa. Today you gratefully had me stay home to reflect on my first ninety days. I did not feel good yesterday, and today I really felt bad. I'm glad I had a chance to reflect. I received three calls today from SAA fellows. Mike, a nurse who still thinks he can be in meetings, be in recovery, then get well and go back out doing the same things he did in the past. He's not ready to commit himself to you yet. Then there is Scott, an atheist. He is in real pain, too. He refuses your name. The last one is Steve; he is in recovery and very committed.

I'm grateful that you have gotten me to see that as time has began to heal me, your love has begun to teach me. I pray for those who are not with you yet. I'm so grateful I am. I know I'm right where I'm suppose to be, on the path I'm suppose to be, with the people I'm suppose to be with. Thank you, Papa. I am humbled at your feet and turn my will over to you. Your loving servant.

Gratitude: Function: noun: The state of being grateful; thankfulness.

"A state of being grateful." Never in my life have I ever felt so thankful for so little, which means so much. This day was my first ninety-day mark acknowledging my addiction. I didn't feel well, and God made it a point for me to be home to get well and reflect on it. I was starting to really hear Him and understand His will for me for this day. This represented a milestone in my recovery. Ninety days of complete abstinence, ninety days of open and honest communication with myself and most importantly, ninety days of pain-free living. I didn't say that I didn't have stress or anxiety. I had plenty of that. However, Papa, with your guidance, love, and support, I have been able to use the tools you have graced me with in order to navigate the waters of confusion and uncertainty. Am I grateful, you might ask? You bet, I'm in *the* state of being grateful.

May 25, 2005

Wow, it's ninety days today for my first SAA meeting. Thank you, Papa. I can be proud. I am proud. I did it with your love and support. Without my faith, I know I would not have been able to survive the pain of my past. Your love and warmth from your arms have cradled me to once again begin to believe in myself and others, one day at a time, hour by hour.

I question some things about my relationship with Lainie and will let you guide me in my answers. I believe you will guide me to the right conclusions when the time is necessary for me to have the questions answered. What will be will be. With your blessings, it will be what it's supposed to be. I love you. Thank you, Papa.

I picked up my ninety-day chip at my meeting and was as proud as a peacock. "This program works if you work it," they say and then they say, "because we're worth it." On this day, I surely felt worth it. I was proud of myself. I stood tall. I had accomplished something for me. I was living life, not just surviving, and all the support of my group and my higher power assisted in making it all possible. I know this. The reason I know this is because if I was left to my own devices, I have proven over and over again I could not handle myself appropriately. Now with recovery, one day at a time, I can turn my will over to a power greater than myself and get the guidance, love, and support to make it all possible. And people wonder why I'm so happy. TyF.

May 26, 2005

Hmm…as I reflected back tonight, I see the "thoughts of horror" that used to rule my life— the drugs, the movies, the unsavory events, the smoking, the dressing, and mostly the confusion. Thank you, Papa. You have brought me to a sanity I never knew. As long as I keep this hideous disease in check, one hour at a time, one day at a time, I can be grateful. For this moment, I am grateful. Thank you, Papa. Your son is kneeling at your feet, awaiting your next command. I love you.

Another day, another blessed twenty-four hours.

May 28, 2005

It's 10:13 P.M. I'm at the house I left in January. Pretty Woman *is on TV. Lainie just went to bed. I'm crying as I write this. The tears are of joy. I've just passed my ninety days in recovery. It hasn't been easy. No one said it would be. Since I left, I admitted I'm a sex addict. I never thought I'd ever do that. To even attach the word "addict" to myself in any way, shape, or form was not something I was willing to do.*

I always attributed the word "addict" to people who were scum, lowlifes, and basically the dregs of the earth. Today I knowingly see those ideals were so far from the truth. Admitting one is an addict takes courage, strength, and a willingness to endure through pain once never thought one could. I'm proud of myself today as I've moved from feeling constant emotional pain to feeling a calmness and inner peace I never thought possible.

God is the one who I give thanks to for bringing me to salvation. Without Him, I would not be here today. I fondly call Him Papa. Papa, I love you for the care, love, warmth, and wisdom you have shared with me in these times as I have embraced my new way of living. Papa, I love you. In these past ninety days, you have shown me miracles I would never had believed possible. The biggest one is that I'm alive. After that, the miracles come in all shapes and sizes. Just typing on these keys after I left in January, to me, is a miracle. Thank you, Papa.

I'm learning who I am. I've learned how to.

This day's entry was written right on the computer. I was spending the night at the house I still owned but since January 5, 2005, was not residing. I was feeling very grateful that night and actually started crying tears of joy, recognizing the accomplishment I had just achieved. It was all so new to me this time, called life. I just wanted to scream and shout how much I loved my higher power, whom I fondly call Papa, and the miracles He has bestowed upon me. The most amazing of them all as you read these words I've written is that I've been in recovery almost two years and live back at my residence with my wife. That's a miracle.

"Recovery is about making memories of miracles, one day at a time."

L.J. Schwartz

May 29, 2005

It's ten-fifteen at night. I've stayed at the house, assisting Lainie after she just had surgery on Friday morning on her left foot. I came back to the house to assist her as she recovers. It's different being here. The "kids" are all running around barking and excited to see me. I have been uncomfortable coming back to the house knowing that Robin would be coming home as well. I haven't faced her yet. Just a week ago, I realized why I get so uncomfortable around Robin in the past. Her personality and actions remind me of how my mother treated me as a child: cold and unresponsive. This is not to say that Robin is a bad person, not at all. These feelings I own alone. As I grew up, my mother was very cold to me, unresponsive, and would shut her bedroom door in my face in order to continue her emotional abuse. Robin, on the other hand, is a warm, loving, private individual. She is not my contemporary and living in our house she requests privacy. This is her life. The way I respond to her lifestyle is my issue. Papa, I'm grateful to you for showing me this insight.

Robin did come home; it was around six o'clock in the evening. She went onto the computer in the Florida room. As I got up from the bed to go out and talk to Robin, I started to get emotional and started to cry. Lainie sat and asked me what was wrong, and I said, "I have a lot of shame and pain associated with having to speak to Robin and I'm sad." I gained my composure and walked out of the bedroom toward the back of the house, where Robin was. I tried not to project my thoughts as I took each step closer to her. A moment later, she was ten feet in front of me. Would I be rejected? Would she speak to me? Was I asking for too much? Thank you, Papa, not only for the strength to stand in the face of this pain, additionally for guiding me to the place I needed to be. As I stood ten feet in front of Robin, I cleared my throat and said, "Hello." To my surprise, she answered back, "Hello." I asked for a moment of her time to talk. She agreed. My stomach was tight, and my eyes welled up with tears of emotion. I said first that I wasn't asking for her forgiveness or to forget what I had done over the years. I apologized for the pain I caused her as she watched me cause pain to her mother.

Then I thanked her for being at the house with her mother after I was gone and how much that meant to me knowing she was there with her mother. She smiled at me and said it was no trouble. I then said to her that for the first time in over twenty-seven years and for the first time in our fifteen-year relationship, the pain has gone away thanks to recovery and most of all to God. With that acknowledgement, streams of tears started down my face as I related my feelings about her mother and the future, one day at a time. I reflected that we are both in therapy and both working on ourselves, emotionally, psychologically, and spiritually. We want to take things very slow. Robin just listened, and I felt I had said enough.

Papa, thank you for the guidance and strength you have instilled in my heart and mind. I turn my will over to you and keep your name with me always to assist those in need. I love you.

This moment scared me. I was going to be face to face with the one person I knew who could shred me emotionally in the blink of an eye. I was so afraid of being rejected. It had been my pattern for so many years: get rejected, feel pain, self-medicate, over and over, year after year. Now was different; I wasn't alone. My soul was supported by my higher power. When I went into the back room to speak to my stepdaughter, I wasn't the same person she remembered who had hurt her mother. I was a humbled person who felt safe for the first time in close to thirty years. I didn't have that internal pain gnawing at my heart. The confusion of my sexuality no longer plagued my inner spirit. I was coming from an entirely different place. A soft-spoken word of love and encouragement from my wife eased the jitters in my belly. I was ready.

Robin and I spoke for no longer than ten minutes, but it seemed longer. Emotionally I broke down and cried while I was halfway through over my hope for the future. Robin was silent, not in a negative way. She was very courteous and allowed me to speak. I appreciated that moment that evening, and I can't thank her enough for all her support.

May 30, 2005

What a beautiful day. I received a call from a fellow in my SAA group, Scott. He called around eleven in the morning. He called to tell me he thinks he now believes in God. He now thinks he belongs to you. I'm so happy to hear that, I cried on the other end of the phone.

I know your glory. I know your guidance. I know your love. I understand everyone comes to you at different times of their lives. I'm glad he thinks he's being with you now. I love you, Papa thank you for your love.

I was so happy for my friend. Fortunately for me, my relationship with God has been really tight. I got all choked up when I heard that he felt that he had finally turned his will over to Him. Believing in a power greater than ourselves is part of the second step of recovery. The other part of that step recognizes that this Higher Power can restore us to sanity. For some people in recovery, this concept seems so foreign; for others it is as natural as breathing. I was one of the very lucky ones; I had a relationship already. Like most addicts, though, when I was in active addiction, I would forget the relationship ever existed. I know now that the relationship never leaves me; I leave it. The truth is my higher power's address never changes; mine does. Once I realized this important fact, my relationship started to flourish to what it is today. I love you, Papa.

June 2, 2005

Another day of sobriety. Ty, Papa. I do know it's not easy. As I was flipping through television channels, HBO had the program Real Sex *on. Just to show you how much my addict wants to come back and take over …I flipped back to that channel three times. I finally said, "Enough." Got up and took a shower, realized I'm allowing this behavior, but now I'm writing about it and feeling much better.*

There is nothing so precious as my sobriety. There is no relationship I hold dearer than the one I have with my Higher Power. There is only one devil on this earth, and he comes with the face of my addiction. Fortunately for me, I have the my Higher Power watching over me, next to me, cradling me every moment I breathe. That evening as I was watching the television, I came to the clear understanding that I have to be on guard constantly, even from watching something as simple as television.

There was a shift in how I would watch television. No longer was it acceptable for me to view programming with overt sexual content such as *Real Sex* or *Taxi Cab Confessions*. Additionally, watching any programming that has any content that dealt with sex or drugs was placed in my middle circle. Movies that had strong sexual content or drug content were now off-limits to me. I was tightening my boundaries. This was to protect me. I was guarding myself, and God was protecting me.

June 5, 2005

It's late; it's already Monday. I've been doing some reading. Lainie called me and apologized to me for actions on Saturday evening regarding a rash conversation. She ended it, "I'm in recovery, too." She's right; she is. Papa, thank you for your love, warmth, and grace on both of us. I know without your love, I would not be here today. You have blessed both of us with your love. I cried when Lainie apologized to me; she made me feel valued and human. She acknowledged that she crossed my boundaries. She said so. I know I felt guarded and challenged. I wasn't a doormat. I miss her. I look forward to being with her soon. I love you, Papa. I'm going to bed.

I'll never forget this day. I was so touched by my wife's presence of mind to apologize to me. She also said that she was taking responsibility of her own pain. She said she no longer was willing to allow me to be responsible for actions she did she directly accused me of causing to her. I was so taken by her actions that I broke down and cried. This was the first time anyone ever made me feel that I had value, like I counted. It's a different feeling than her agreeing with me in a specific topic of conversation. It's about being acknowledged that you matter in life and the other person is going to do their part in making you feel worthwhile. I didn't feel this good even on the day of my wedding. I finally felt the depth of my wife's love for me that moment.

June 7, 2005

Papa, today is a special day. Today I am doing my seventh Breathwork session. I feel really good with a lot of things. Later on…Well, I was right; this session did hold true to my statement of being special. Today I did my first entry into past lives. To say it was interesting would be an understatement, to say the least. Incredible relates better. As Caren would say, I'm here in this life to fulfill a correction. Today I believe I was shown what one might entail. I'm not saying that the work I did today will be the whole correction. However, it is I believe either the portal or an entrance into the doorway of what the correction is about.

My Breathwork started like the first six sessions, slowly at first, then picking up speed and intensity as the energy started to flow through my system. After a few bursts of energy from my lower back coming out, I felt a sharpening pain below my heart and toward the left. This pain did not move. It was unlike other energy in the past. It stayed in the area for longer than the usual time. My body began to move in an unnatural way. I moved in a way that seemed to illustrate pain of different sort. What I soon found out was that I had entered into my first past life experience. The body movements were due to trauma.

I was a scout in the Calvary of the United States Army; the date was early to mid-1800s. What I saw around me astonished me. I could clearly see a fort in the distance complete with canons and a lot of fence border with spiked tops. The fence had to be at least fifteen feet tall. The fort was in the distance; I was on a ridge in the woods. I had been shot below the heart and to the left. It would prove to be a mortal wound. Above me stood an Indian; he was watching me die. He walked away as I lay there and took my last breath. I watched as my left leg slowly slid to the ground as I exhaled my last breath. I was dead. I rose above my body, I rose above the whole scene. I only remember a white puffy essence, nothing concrete. I saw a figure dressed in period clothing, I saw her eyes. The eyes were those of my current wife. We looked at each other, then turned and walked away. Shortly thereafter, a sense of a lesson appeared to me in my mind. The lesson from this past life was that anger doesn't need to create REVENGE. I joined the Calvary to revenge my wife's death at the hands of the Indians.

As the Breathwork session continued, a second past life appeared. I was an older wealthy businessman in his late seventies. Before I go into it, I need to state the lesson I got from my first past life, as I mentioned, dealt with revenging my wife's death. The REVENGE brought me to her as I was killed because of it. ANGER/REVENGE show up as a lesson learned for a correction in this life. My mother is a very angry person. She was the mirror for my past life of anger. I wanted to get revenge for the way she took my father away from me. They were horrible thoughts. I see now that correction. Now I also see how ANGER/REVENGE align in my life. The other past life's lesson was BITTERNESS toward money. In this life, I was bitter at my father for not making arrangements prior to his *death to make sure my birthright was protected. I now under-stand this lesson and money seems to have a whole new way of showing up. I love you, Papa. You are my guide, my light, my life. I humbly serve you.*

This day, this moment proved to be one of the most impor-tant days in my life. First, there was the epiphany of my addiction, then this day ranks second. Few times in person's life does an event impact someone as much as this day did for me.

In the journal entry above, I described an event that even to me is still astonishing, but it happened. For me it confirmed my relationship with my now-current wife and has led me to believe that this lifetime is all predestined. Even the pages of this book are part of a bigger plan that has been set for me to follow. I've come to realize the reason I am here is exactly what these pages speak. I am the advocate my eternal Father wants me to become, the voice of many who suffer in darkness around the globe. I am their voice.

In the second past life, I talk about the lesson of bitterness re-garding money. This came about as the wealthy businessman I was in that period sat painfully by and watched my wife pass away from injuries suffered from a car accident. The times were the 1940s; my wife and I were in our car driving when all of sudden at an intersection, I was broadsided by another car. I was thrown from the car, and my wife suffered horrible injuries. I sat and cried as she slowly passed away from her injuries while she was in the hospital. I became very bitter because with all the money I had I could not buy the necessary care to keep her alive. I never re-married. I became more or less a recluse with the memory of my wife on my mind until the day I died in a chair, at my home, in my library. Once again I rose above my scene. This time I saw my father standing off to the side. It was a very emotionally dif-ficult time for me.

The lesson of bitterness regarding money could be seen very clearly as it transferred to my life today. When my father died, there were no provisions for my birthright to be protected from my mother, who claimed there was no will. I know my father had a will because he told me so. I had become very bitter about money and had felt that I was robbed of my birthright. The lesson taught me to appreciate money in a whole new perspective. Money flows to me because of my relationship with my Higher Power. He takes care of me, I shall not want. In the past I was acting like a greedy, spoiled brat. That is not the way to attract money in life. Now that I am guided by a different source, I do not want. In a way, my father did me the greatest justice in showing me the truth of my actions, without which I would have never learned this lesson. Thank you, Papa.

June 13, 2005

It's been almost seven days since I last wrote. I've been on a little mental vacation, not to say I haven't been with you in my life. I've been processing what occurred in my last Breathwork session. Papa, I just got very sleepy; it's late. The point is I love you and just wanted you to know.

It may sound redundant how much I thank my Higher Power for loving, supporting, and guiding me. The truth is what I have found being grateful is a huge part of staying in sobriety. His presence in my daily life assists me moment to moment. I believe I am very lucky to have this type of relationship with my Higher Power. Some people hear about such relationships and wish they too could create one for themselves. My hope is that those who seek His love will find Him deep in their hearts. He truly does create miracles out of thin air. I know; I'm one of them.

June 15, 2005

Wow...Papa, I just found out why I'm in such a funk. I've been feeling very slow like a turtle. I haven't felt like working much on designs. My birthday is in three weeks, and I'm entering into a very emotional state. It's eleven o'clock at night. I think the truth is as I lose balance, I start to shut down. I bring it upon myself. I believe pinpointing this is very important.

Thank you, Papa, for your guidance. I know I don't ask for the help I should. Can you please forgive me for being unsure

*of how to ask? I'm so frightened, Papa. I'm okay. I hear you say
I'll be fine. Thank you. I know you're with me. Thank you. I
love you so much. You've helped me grow, you always help me
grow. I'm crying tears of joy for my relationship with you. Today
I grew a little more than yesterday, progress one day at a time.*

*Today I called Lainie and apologized to her for blowing her
off whenever she tried to assist me with insights regarding business. Today what I realized is she is one of my most beloved
cheerleaders for success. I advised her that from now on I will
keep an open mind to her suggestions. I will use her information as another part of analysis. It doesn't mean I have to use
it. I just have to respect her opinion if I ask for it. Papa, I feel
a lot better since I spent time with you.*

They say that hindsight is twenty-twenty. What I've found is
something new, insight. The SAA program has given me so
much. The ability to take the time analyzing my relationships has
been one of the greatest fruits I've been able to cultivate. On this
day in particular, I grew once more, emotionally and psychologically. I found out once again that others can help me. For so long,
I feared people to assist me. It was part of my isolation. No one's
opinion was greater than mine. Thanks to you, Papa, I've learned
that my own wife is not my enemy. She cares for me deeply.
When she gives me suggestions, she is looking out for my best interest. What I've experienced since this day has only been God's
grace regarding my relationship with my wife. Our marriage has
grown so much. Papa, I love you.

June 19, 2005, Father's Day

*Thank you, Papa. My heart is lighter knowing that your love
is in my heart. I've finalized a new tattoo for myself. It speaks
volumes for me and it honors you; it will forever and ever.
"NEVER ALONE." I know and feel it's perfect for me. I'm
not alone; I have you in my life, today, tomorrow, and forever.
Thank you, Papa—I am your humble servant.*

*Later that day…Papa, today I've honored you. I tattooed
my right arm with the slogan "NEVER ALONE." Like I said*

earlier, forever and for eternity, I am not alone. I know you are in my life. My tattoo represents my commitment to myself and to you in knowing this. It is an absolute; however, it is not tempting fate. I know you are with me. I know you love me, and I know you are in my heart eternally. Thank you, Papa. I love you.

Never Alone

I was told that using absolutes while I journal or speak could be hazardous to my sobriety. It has to do with tempting fate. "I'll never do that again" or "I always do that." These are examples of absolutes that challenge fate that are used daily by people in recovery. Fate is tempted to miss whatever is said or written that would "never" be done again, giving guilt a chance to set in to our psyche. When guilt has that opportunity to run rampant in our thoughts, shame usually follows. This is the time when I would want to act out to medicate myself from the shame I was feeling regarding whatever activity I felt guilty about because I promised myself I would never do the action ever again. That's how the vicious cycle would continue. I act out, feel guilty, shame would follow, then I'd act out again to cover up the shame. This cycle has at times gone on for hours or days at a time, sometimes even months or years depending on what the activity was. However long it would continue was not as bad as the harmfulness the action might be. It becomes really clear now why when someone is in recovery why it's not a good idea to use absolutes in speaking or journaling. What I found with this tattoo slogan was a loophole in that theory because as sure as you are reading these words, my Higher Power is with me and always will be. Hence I tattooed it on my arm so I'd never forget the truth about my Higher Power's love and support of me. That's an absolute I can count on.

June 21, 2005

I have a dilemma. My wife is upset with me regarding my roommate and her view on my being allowed to have my wife over to my apartment. I will speak to my sponsor about it and pray to God for guidance. Okay, I spoke to Dave about my situation regarding my roommate. I've never seen him so agitated over something as he was. He brought to my attention that my roommate, being a spiritual healer, should recognize how important it is NOT to subject someone less fortunate than her spiritually, in a cruel manner. God would not approve of her selfish behavior.

Rather she should open her arms to Lainie and allow her to heal through healing ways. I listened to Dave; it made sense. I'm not making my roommate wrong. I feel it is an area she needs to grow in. It's just an observation. I love you, Papa, for your everlasting love and support.

When one discusses growth, it can come in many forms. For me this time, it came as emotional growth. I was being challenged and knew it. I was at a critical point in my growth for sure. The difference was I was ready for the challenge. I had support on my side as well as my higher power. There really was no competition; I was being groomed to move on. I chose my battles very carefully, and this one I was going to fight.

I know in the past my relationship between my roommate and my wife was bad at best. My roommate never wanted to speak to my wife or even meet her and was not allowing my wife to visit where I lived. In the early days of my recovery, I believed my roommate had just cause for keeping my wife at bay. But as the months drifted by and my relationship with my wife started to grow in a very healthy way, I started to see the truth in how my roommate treated my wife. It was unhealthy. My sponsor had made a very rational comment to me when he stated that anyone who is doing spiritual work knows how important healthy relationships are to the person in need of healing. Then why was I being subjected to such behavior I couldn't understand. I didn't make my roommate wrong; I knew in my heart it was just an area that she needed to grow, in her own time. My fight was far from over.

July 2, 2005

Good morning, Papa. Thank you for this beautiful morning, I'm going to the beach before I go to my meeting at ten-thirty. Papa, I have been processing what happened on June twenty-first regarding Lainie, and I've come to see you have guided me to defend myself. I am a person. I have rights. I am a good person, I have honest thoughts. I am a worthy person, I deserve to be happy. I now am speaking my feelings even to those people

I care about. I'm not being vicious, rather in a kind, loving manner that represents you. I love you, Papa, and know I'm never alone.

You can hear how far I have grown from the words I use to describe my feelings. These feelings are the result of accomplishment in my SAA program. The program has enlightened me to my own self-worth and value. It has guided me in understanding the most important relationship of all: the one with myself. From this new vantage point and with the relationship with my higher power, I have been able to speak my feelings from a whole new level representing my true self. I can stand strong with the tools I've learned over the past twenty-two months and know when my boundaries are being challenged that I can defend myself intellectually without having to lash out. This is recovery in action, a far cry from my days in addiction. Papa, I can't thank you enough for your undying love and support.

July 6, 2005

Papa, thank you for another glorious day, thank you for your guidance. Today I made a decision, after careful consideration, to stop going to my men's group, which meets on Wednesdays in the afternoon from twelve-fifteen until one-forty-five. I did so after speaking to my sponsor, my therapist, and to you. Dave advised me that since I'm focusing in on my business and this cuts into my workday, I'm going to my therapist, Caren. I speak to him every day, going to four SAA meetings a week, journaling, calling a support team; it's a natural tendency to move on. I requested from Caren to change my appointment time as well. I'm honoring my "being," my worth, and my basic needs for me.

Thank you, Papa, for your love and guidance.

This was a big step for me. It was the right move. I was starting to gain my balance as I was walking, similar to a baby taking his first steps. I was taking control of my own destiny. Of course, I have no control over anything or anyone and I'm still powerless over my disease, but I'm growing emotionally and spiritually and you can see it as clear as day.

The men's group was a support when I first became a member; however, as time went on, the type of atmosphere this group offered I found was not as supportive to my needs any longer. The decision I made to stop going was done after carefully thinking it through as opposed to the rash thinking when I was in addiction. I had made a good choice.

July 10, 2005

Papa, thank you for loving me unconditionally even when my thoughts were deviant. I've asked you to take all of my thoughts away, and you have. I've filled up my space with good, healthy thoughts, happy thoughts, and ideas. I thank you for your forgiveness of all of my sins I have caused to myself and others. I've turned my will over to you unconditionally, and I do each day as I arise. I know in my heart of hearts I will never be abandoned by you. You have given me guidance to make the right choices for myself. You have restored me to sanity. I have learned to understand myself better. I have learned to forgive myself for my past indulgences. I know your love has kept me safe and in recovery. I know that my belief in your power and love for me allows each day to unfold graciously with dignity, honor, and integrity. I love you, Papa.

The third step in the SAA program states that I "made a decision to turn my will and my life over to the care of God as I understood God." On this day, it's easy to see in plain English I have followed my heart and led it right to the banks of the river of recovery. With God as my teacher, I was willing to be the student. I have felt his love and support before, and it's clear to me I am unconditionally being kept by His heart. I kneel at His feet and have asked what His will for me is and in a dream, He told me to write this book. He has restored me to sanity from the life of lies and deceit. Papa, for all your warmth, support, and love, I humbly serve you. My recovery has been the greatest accomplishment I have ever attempted for myself. I have become proud of myself; I have integrity and live a life full of dignity. This is my recovery in action.

July 11, 2005

Papa, thank you for your guidance today. I had a rough time at a job due to my addiction. I did the design while I was in my addiction and never re-measured it. Thanks to you, my SAA group "Promises" and the Serenity Prayer allowed me to just laugh and grow from the experience. I know I'm not bad and wrong. It's about how I handled the situation, which used to baffle me. Today, I just handled it. I love you, Papa. Every day has been and can be a day of education.

What a difference recovery makes. When I realized the design was done while I was in an addiction, it explained why the mistakes existed. In the past, I would have just blown off finishing the job. I would have told my client a lie and left the home in order to go act out. Not this day. I was so proud of myself for pushing through the mistakes, resolving the issues, and finishing the job completely. I had grown again, one moment at a time.

July 19, 2005

Papa, today has been a mentally tough day, and I don't know why. I've been having thoughts about my past life and how it would feel to act out again. I know it's wrong and would kill me. Why am I still having these thoughts? I just want them to go away. I called my sponsor; he did not answer. I'm not alone, so here I am. I know I am powerless over my addiction and that my life had become unmanageable. I'm asking for your guidance. I've turned my will over to you.

Recovery is a process; it just doesn't magically appear in our lives. As addicts we, of course, want everything yesterday. We're not used to waiting for anything. Our lives were filled with instant gratification. On this day, I was experiencing a very stressful time. I was under pressure to get my jobs completed and was having issues with a neighbor who lived in the complex. As you might have noticed, I stopped writing in my journal on a daily basis. This was a grounding exercise; it kept me on track like a commitment. In recovery, addicts learn to become commitment oriented. This keeps us from letting ourselves fall prey to our addict in our heads with comments like "See? You can't even keep a commitment" or "Just another failure." These thoughts can erode our self-esteem into thinking we aren't worthy of our recovery, a sad commentary in any addict's life. This day was just one that I allowed my addiction to rear its talkative little mouth and fell prey into believing the rhetoric I was creating in my head. I didn't act out that day, but I was not in a good place mentally. This is when making phone calls to other members of the program for support is a key to keeping one's sobriety. If all else fails, just follow directions—"DON'T ACT OUT."

August 2, 2005

Papa, tonight I write to you while I use the Bible as my support. I never knew how much I'd like to read it. I'm reading Proverbs from the Old Testament. As you already know it, it is the written word of wisdom from King Solomon, son of King David. I wanted a mentor to teach me about becoming a man, not that I'm going to repeat the verses, verse by verse, rather learn the verses' true meaning and try to incorporate your laws into my daily life. I love you and I know you feel the same, TyF. Your loving son, me.

This was a magical time in my life. I had never read from the Bible ever in my life. This was new territory for me. Growing up in a non-religious Jewish home, we rarely even went to synagogue. We did observe some of the traditional holidays until my mother stopped cooking for me at thirteen. Then I was not invited to holiday activities any longer. Basically after I had my bar mitzvah, all of my religious study stopped. My father was not a mentor for me, nor was my brother or any male in my life from there on. I just didn't trust anyone. Now fast forward to August

2, 2005. I was handed a Bible, and it was suggested to me to read Proverbs in order to learn how to conduct myself as a man in life. In essence, creating the source of a mentor for me in my life, a move I recommend to all of my sponsees in recovery. There is no better advice I could learn than something that is thousands of years old and has stood the test of time. Papa, as my teachers' teacher, I thank you every day for the guidance I receive as I listen to it. My hope is that every addict learns to commit Proverbs to their life as they walk their own paths. Its wisdom speaks to all men regardless of ethnic background or religious beliefs. I can tell you without a shadow of a doubt, I've grown into a better person because of Proverbs. I had found my mentor.

August 5, 2005

Papa, I feel I have lost my sobriety due to talking to a "friend." I had to tell her I could no longer speak to her. I feel stressed, I feel I have let myself get stressed. I feel I have not handled a job correctly and let the stress of that job rule my emotions—a situation that used to baffle me. This is not good. I have retreated into a shell. Papa, please assist me with these feelings of uncertainty.

Today I woke up from bad dreams, bad dreams about drugs, sex, and suicide. I wanted to go back to my disease to die. Why would I want to do this? Why do I allow the shame of the past control my present? Why do I have such pain? I believe I am not being honest with myself regarding how I ended the relationship with Wendy. She is not a healthy person for me to have in my life. Why am I drawn to this? I feel as though there are entities in my mind trying to control me. I'm very scared, I'm frightened. I'm so afraid of going backwards that I feel going backwards in order to end the insanity of being afraid of going back. This way I'll never have to worry about it again because I'll be dead. Papa, I don't want to die. I feel I'm going insane.

"Somebody get the monkey off my back." I crashed and burned hard. The Saturday before, at ten o'clock in the morning,

I got a call from this interest intrigue friend of mine. We had a long history together, and she knew my story for eleven years or so. She enabled my double life as an addict and indulged in my addiction. Over the years, my delusions surrounding our friendship drove me to allow myself to deepen a double life. After I got into recovery, I came to see how this relationship was toxic to my growth; I had to end it. I never called her, and months had passed since we spoke. Then out of the blue on an early Saturday morning, I got the call. Impulsively, I answered my phone. She blindsided me with her talk of sexual innuendoes and within ten seconds, I lost my sobriety. I was entangled, once again in a web of sexual chatter, that after the call had ended the only thing I had to show for it was a wet towel that I used to clean myself after I had masturbated.

The reality of this day absolutely scared me to death. I had five months of sobriety thus far. My mind went into a tizzy. What do I do now? All of a sudden, the thought of lying entered back into my mind. I had taken back my "control" in my life. Who was I kidding? I once again felt doomed. None of this stopped me from picking up that phone and making a repeat call back to my cohort. The thought that runs through my mind is an old recovery line, "One is too many, and a thousand times is never enough." That described me. I was off to the races, chasing after that high over and over again. I was now ten minutes into my acting out; no one knew my mind had reverted back to my old habits of lies and deceit. My wife was only fifty feet away from me and had no idea I had broken my sobriety. I choose not to tell her; it was my secret. Once again I was in my double life. The guilt and shame started in on me, and I felt lower than low. I was in a boxing match with myself, beating myself up bad. Where to run? The pain of my disease hit like a ton of bricks all from one little mistake. I was back in my addiction knee-deep, and all I wanted to do was crawl out and hide.

August 8, 2005

Papa, please watch over me as I sleep. Please have your heavenly angels watch over my bed as I sleep. Papa, please give Lainie the health she so deserves and for me, please restore me to sanity. Thankfully you are there when I feel bad and when these bad times are with me. I know you are holding me in your warmth. I humbly am on my knees, begging for your mercy to spare me the pain I feel and to take me away from Satan's grip. He's a liar. They are all lies being told to me. I know as my phone rings with business that you afford me peace from financial despair. I know you help me. I know I am an addict, I accept. To fall down and slip, I accept. To hear Satan's voice disguised as your voice asking me to come out and play is driving me nuts. I miss my old ways, but I do know it will kill me.

I'm now in my eighth day of relapse and I'm begging my Higher Power to relieve the pain from my mind. I feel I'm going insane and can't stop the insanity. I still haven't told my sponsor, and I'm paying the price of isolation. I felt as though I was on a patch of ice and every time I tried to stand up, I would fall right back down. I kept hearing the chatter in my mind, the lies about my behaviors, and allowed myself to fall back into some of my old habits. I began to beg for mercy but forgot how I got back to my original place of sobriety. At no time did I admit I was powerless over my addiction and that my life had become unmanageable, the first of the twelve steps. I hadn't humbled myself enough yet. I was blinded by my desires to still want my old ways. I had found an easier, softer way for my recovery, and no one could tell me otherwise, nor did I tell anyone. The pain was becoming unbearable.

August 10, 2005

Today is a beautiful day. I've decided, after speaking to Dave, that I wanted to move back home. I've had my concerns about coming home. Dave suggested I move back because I needed to handle any and all issues I was having at home, not apart from Lainie. It's funny, Dave reminds me of Marc, except for the fact that I can tell Dave anything and, as my sponsor, he understands and doesn't judge me. Marc just loves me and doesn't understand me. It's okay. That's just Marc.

I told Kari I was leaving and going back to Lainie, and I know in her heart she is only hoping for the best for me. The truth is I wasn't. The truth is I want to be home. I love Lainie, I love myself. I know I belong with Lainie. I am a man in recovery. I know God is with me and I owe my life to Him. I humbly will do what I need to follow His guidance. I owe Kari a thank-you and a half for the support, love, and guidance she has shown me over these last seven months and five days. She has been an earthly angel along with Caren, sent to assist in my recovery and guidance. For that and her love, I will always have a place in my heart for her.

Kari, I love you for your guidance back to my Father's feet repeatedly reminding me who I am in the world. For giving me the gift of wisdom through Proverbs to become the man I've wanted to become but never knew how.

Proverbs 1
33 "Whoever listens to me will live in safety
and be at ease, without fear of harm."

You have opened my eyes and soul to the right path for my heart and mind.

Proverbs 1
1 The proverbs of Solomon son of David, king of Israel:
2 for attaining wisdom and discipline;
    for understanding words of insight;
3 for acquiring a disciplined and prudent life,
    doing what is right and just and fair;
4 for giving prudence to the simple,
    knowledge and discretion to the young-
5 let the wise listen and add to their learning,
    and let the discerning get guidance-
6 for understanding proverbs and parables,
    the sayings and riddles of the wise.
7 The fear of the LORD is the beginning of knowledge,
    but fools despise wisdom and discipline.

This has become the catalyst for my returning to my home. The only one I ever need to listen to in the future is the one who has never left me alone. Papa, I love you and know you are there for me and know even in times of trouble you are teaching me. I thank you and know you are the only one to bring me back to sanity. I turn my heart and will over to you. I love you and will follow your commands.

From this day forward, one day at a time, I know I am forgiven and know I have the ability to learn all I need for my future. I know that my past does not make my future. That my self-destructive ways do not give solid footing to Lainie's confidence and that running away from my issues doesn't build a strong character. Keeping the teachings of my Father close at heart will give the guidance and love I'll need to overcome. Ty, Papa.

I called Dave and finally told him about my loss of sobriety. I was in tears, I hurt so badly. Things were still out of hand; I had acted out again that day. I felt so ashamed of my behavior, and the guilt from the lies was so painful. Dave said he knew something was up with me. He said I had been acting strange. I couldn't understand how he could still care about me. I thought I had perpetrated a mortal sin. Dave, to my surprise, was extremely understanding. He said he's never seen anyone come into recovery with such a conviction to recovery as I had and that I should be proud of myself for the time I had amassed. He wasn't wrong. I did manage to amass five months and five days of sobriety before I had my first relapse and acted out. What I was starting to understand was the true relationship between a sponsor and a sponsee. Dave was my guide. He didn't judge me; he understood me. He had walked in my shoes in his own journey and was sharing his wisdom in order to comfort me. I wasn't used to someone caring for me when I did something wrong. On the contrary, I was usually berated very badly. I would be going to my next meeting and picking up a white chip.

Additionally Dave and I discussed my situation of me still living outside my own home. I had more than understood that I really missed my wife. I was so in love with her. Dave had pointed out that I had come a long way from the beginning days of recovery. He suggested that since we both professed our love for each other and that I had truly grown into my own person that going back home should be considered. Lainie had asked me, too. I thought it would be okay. That day I called Lainie and asked if she still was ready for me to come back home. Once again God's grace-filled hand had touched my head and she said yes. It was a beautiful night.

August 11, 2005

Good morning, Papa. I have never been so happy to rise on to a new day as I have this morning. Your guidance last night left me with the new insight I came to this morning. I had a really bad night's sleep last night due to the supplement energy drink I drank before I went and worked out. I finally got to sleep at around 5:00 A.M., waking up at 7:15 A.M. without acting out. I prayed and prayed through the night for you to watch over me and keep me safe like Kari had shown me. This morning I reviewed the thoughts that I was having. They were the same bad dreams I was having Saturday, July 30. I even traced these thought patterns back further to when I binged on cocaine or abused my Ritalin medication. The same bad dreams or even awake feelings I would have all dealt with me using drugs and in negative sexual encounters. The encounters I would feel extremely shameful and guilty about. Last night, I again felt as if I was going insane. Thank you, Papa, for the readings I was reviewing in Proverbs. It was you who pointed out to me in, Proverbs 1:5:

> "Let the wise listen and add to their learning,
>   and let the discerning get guidance."

Through your guidance, I humbly awoke with the understanding of why my mind felt like it was going crazy. I love you. Thank you for the new teaching that I received today. I will treasure it and share it upon the earth for all to hear who are willing to take you LORD.

What a horrible night I had. I was still living at the apartment. I was alone. I drank an energy drink earlier that evening and worked out. It was the first time using this drink. To my surprise, it created the same type of issues in my dreams as if I was awake while high on cocaine or Ritalin. I was a mess. My brain was working overtime with dreams about sex and drugs. I couldn't fall asleep until five in the morning. Throughout the night, I got up almost in tears to have God take away these insane thoughts running in my head. I thought about acting out again and again. I kept turning it all over to God over and over until I finally fell asleep. This was a very frightening experience. I am so blessed to have such a wonderful relationship with my Higher Power. Without His love and support, I know I would not have gotten through that night. I know for a fact I wasn't alone.

August 14, 2005

I had a nice weekend with Lainie. We worked together as a team. I'm sitting in the second bedroom now as I type this. I'm very grateful, Papa, for the time we spend together. I have been listening to PROVERBS. I wish I had this to listen to when I was sixteen or so. I'm not sure it would have made any difference. I'm quite clear my head would not have been clear enough to hear the message. I'm clear that NOW is the time. I, the student, was ready and King Solomon, my teacher, appeared. Thank you, Papa. I'm filled with emotion at this moment. My eyes fill with tears. I'm becoming a humble student, and my hopes are to dwell upon the house of my Lord and never leave Him again…These truths Solomon teaches to me:

Proverbs 1
[5] Get wisdom, get understanding;
   do not forget my words or swerve from them.
[6] Do not forsake wisdom, and she will protect you;
   love her, and she will watch over you.
[7] Wisdom is supreme; therefore get wisdom.
   Though it cost all you have, get understanding.
[8] Esteem her, and she will exalt you;
   embrace her, and she will honor you.

⁹ She will set a garland of grace on your head
  and present you with a crown of splendor."
¹⁰ Listen, my son, accept what I say,
  and the years of your life will be many.
¹¹ I guide you in the way of wisdom
  and lead you along straight paths.
¹² When you walk, your steps will not be hampered;
  when you run, you will not stumble.
¹³ Hold on to instruction, do not let it go;
  guard it well, for it is your life

will forever change my life. I'm not looking to just hear words. I'm going to live these truths. Papa, this is your request. I hear you. I feel your love surround me. I will be your messenger. I know in my heart this is what I am to do. Papa, why me, though? Why do request of me to be your messenger? I hear you. I will go. I love you and will obey your commands.

I had an incredible weekend with my wife. I was glad I moved back in. Thank you, Papa, for all your guidance, love, and support. Your humble son.

This concludes the entries into my journal. I never kept a journal after I moved back in with my wife. I guess it closed a chapter of my life.

Ten days to the day, I moved back out of the house and went back to the apartment. What I found out was I wasn't ready to move back into my house; I still had issues I wasn't aware of that I had to resolve. Who would have thought that moving back to my own house would stir up unresolved issues? First, there was the issue with going outside in the backyard. There was so much history I had with acting out and the backyard that I felt paralyzed to go out back. For years this part of my house was littered with hours of delusions, no matter what time of day or time of year. The history was negative.

Then there were the feelings dealings with reestablishing my relationship with my wife on a more permanent basis. All the people who were on my wife's side—my stepdaughter, an ex-sister-in-law, etc.—had ill feelings toward me moving back in. It was hard not to feel "less than" or "unwanted" due to their heartfelt feelings. I understood and worked at not letting them in, but it was still difficult.

I called my sponsor, Dave, and went over everything that had been going on, and he assisted me with words of wisdom. Then that next weekend, Dave came over to my apartment and helped me move out permanently. He said that whatever issues I had at home, I needed to resolve them there and with Lainie. It was a long day.

Looking back, I wouldn't change anything I did while I lived apart from my wife. I became a man. I grew emotionally and psychologically. I became my own person. I didn't need my wife to make my identity; I had my own. Recovery really opened my eyes to a world I had never seen before. Even though right at that time in my life I was in active addiction, no one could take away the five months of sobriety I had earned. The feelings I was feeling were all tied to moving back and with my work. I had become very anxious with work and handling my relationship with my wife as well as continuing to relapse. I hung in there. I wasn't willing to let go. What I came across next floored me. My wife had been feeling like she had been walking on eggshells living with me. While at the bookstore, she came upon a book, *Stop Walking on Eggshells,* opened it up and, within a couple of pages, knew she was on to something. The book's subtitle was regarding the condition called Borderline Personality Disorder, or BPD, a mental disorder that has no known cure but is manageable with medication.

Lainie didn't show me or speak to me about the book right away until she read it. Meanwhile, my conditioned worsened until I felt that I was completely drained emotionally. I was begging God to help me. By a stroke of luck, we had found a doctor, a psychiatrist who was new to the area and an expert in the area of BPD. I got an appointment and sat through a battery of tests until he came to his conclusion. I did, in fact, have BPD, which explained my feelings of loss of identity and being anxious. Now all I needed was an appointment with a doctor in my health network, which I got for a month away.

It was now the end of September, and I was still in my addiction. No matter how many meetings I was going to in a week, no matter how many times I spoke to my sponsor, no matter how much step work I did, I still found it difficult to not be impulsive and then become compulsive. Dave, my sponsor, I felt was losing faith in me and told me I needed to get myself on track. I pleaded with him that I was doing all that I could and didn't understand why after all I did I still couldn't control myself. He was as perplexed as I was. Then the bottom fell out. On October 3, 2005, at five o'clock in the morning, I sat on the end of our bed and cried as I spoke to an operator on a crisis hotline affiliated with the health network to which I belong. I explained my feelings of insanity, anxiousness, impulsivity, and compulsivity and told her that I needed an emergency appointment with a psychiatrist or I was going to have to be placed in an institution. By the grace of God, by nine in the morning, I had an appointment with a doctor right in my area, an appointment that changed my life.

You have to understand what BPD is to understand why the appointment changed my life. According to the American Psychiatric Association (APA), the incidence of BPD is nearly that of schizophrenia and bipolar disorder combined, which equates to about six million people. The DSM–IV definition reads as follows:

"A pervasive pattern of instability of interpersonal relationships, self-image and affects (moods) and marked impulsivity beginning by early adulthood and present in a variety of contexts, as indicated by five or more of the following:

1. Frantic efforts to avoid real or imagined abandonment.
2. A pattern of unstable and intense interpersonal relationships characterized by alternating between extremes of idealization and devaluation.
3. Identity disturbance: markedly and persistently unstable self-image or sense of self.
4. Impulsivity in at least two areas that are potentially self-damaging (e.g., spending, sex, substance abuse, shoplifting, reckless driving, binge eating).
5. Recurrent suicidal behavior, gestures, or threats or self-mutilating behavior.

6. Affective instability due to a marked reactivity of mood (e.g., intense episodic dysphoria, irritability, or anxiety usually lasting a few hours and rarely more than a few days). [Dysphoria is the opposite of euphoria. It's a mixture of depression, anxiety, rage, and despair.]
7. Chronic feelings of emptiness.
8. Inappropriate, intense anger or difficulty controlling anger.
9. Transient, stress-related paranoid ideation or severe dissociative symptoms."

After reading the definition, one can understand my joy to have a diagnosis when living life was so riddled with confusion, anxiety, and anger. I was so glad to have been at the doctor's office. I was finally going to be given medication to stabilize my erratic emotional behavior. I truly felt I was going insane. I was scared and frightened of my own behavior. Just imagine for a moment that you are fine one moment and you fly off the handle in rage at your partner or that you keep feeling like putting the end of a barrel of a gun in your mouth and pulling the trigger. In my last few days before the doctor's appointment, I almost splattered my brains across our bedroom, I was in such a state of dysphoria. Today I can only describe my medication as the saving grace of my life. My Higher Power saw fit to place the doctors in my life to assist me and regulate my disorder.

For me this was a missing part of the puzzle to my behaviors. Not to take anything away from my SAA program. The plain, true fact is I am a sex addict; however, what it states in the passage "How It Works" is that even people with psychological and emotional disorders can recover if the have the capacity to be rigorously honest. I am one of "those" people. I'm an ADHD adult, I have bipolar disorder, and to top it off, I'm BPD. Thankfully today I have my medications and my program; this is the formula for success for me. Thank you, Papa.

The evening of October 3, 2005, I made it back to my SAA meeting. I walked into the room and sat along the front wall. I kept looking at the ground, I was so emotionally spent. Then I raised my hand to share. The moment I opened my mouth, a flood of emotions hit me like a ton of bricks. I figuratively hit my knees and began begging God for mercy, I was in so much pain. I told a story of heinous behavior and kept begging for God to take away the pain. I was broken; He had finally broke me. I was willing to turn my will over to Him completely, no easier, softer way anymore, just one hundred percent devotion to my Higher Power. I kept crying, I was an emotional wreck. That moment I felt warmth and security come over me and cradle me with love. I knew He had heard my prayers. I was extremely grateful. Fast forward to this day, October 3, 2007, I have had two years of abstinence and sobriety from all sexual activities except to be with my wife and feel so humbled by God's grace. I am so grateful. The program works, if you work it, so work it, I know I'm worth it. I now sponsor six different people; I do service by chairing meetings, and I have a great sponsor who gets who I am. I work the steps hard because I found out that recovery is found through the steps. This is a program of rediscovering who we each are. It's like the perfect parent guiding us toward solitude and serenity.

Since regaining my sobriety that night of October 3, 2005, I have had the distinct pleasure of personal miracles that still amaze me. My marriage has grown strong; our love for each other has built a wonderful home full of serenity and hope. Hope for a future filled with continued love and support. I have settled into a field of work that afford me a good income and plenty of job stability. I've even gone back to school to enrich my life. None of these gifts would have ever been possible if I was still in my addiction.

I will forever be in debt to this program, which has turned me into a man of honor, a man of integrity, and a man of compassion. It's my hope that anyone who follows my footsteps through the program or any program of recovery gains as much joy and happiness as I have had the privilege to have. This has been my journey to freedom.

What Others Are Saying…

"While reading this book was enlightening for me, the most wonderful benefit of all was the way it helped me to interact with my family member. It also gave me a perspective of understanding, so I may be there to help him. Having this addiction does not take away from the loving and caring person who happens to be afflicted with this or any other addiction."

Bonnie H.

"In this eye-opening memoir, L.J. Schwartz shines a bright light on one of the darkest corners of the human condition: sex addiction. With stunning clarity and unflinching candor, Schwartz leads the reader on his harrowing personal journey—from a childhood rocked by abuse through years of compulsive sexual behavior and ultimately to a place of peace, resolution, and sobriety. Along the way, he provides a singular perspective on the many facets of addiction and points the way toward treatment and recovery for millions of Americans facing similar afflictions. In this deeply personal and affecting memoir, Schwartz delivers an invaluable contribution to our understanding of addictive behaviors and makes a significant addition to the growing body of literature on addiction medicine. A triumph!"

Nick Tate, Fort Lauderdale Sun-Sentinel